VOLUME
# 2
# SKILLS & KNOWLEDGE INVESTMENT PORTFOLIO

## Pathway

## to

# Success

*Carol Carter*

■

*Carol Ozee*

■

*Sarah Kravits*

Pearson
Custom
Publishing

Cover art: "Road to Sun Through Video Monitor," by Steven Hunt / The Image Bank.

Printed in the United States of America

This manuscript was supplied camera-ready by the author(s).

10 9 8 7 6 5 4 3

*Please visit our web site at www.pearsoncustom.com*

ISBN 0–536–01783–2

BA 990150

 **PEARSON CUSTOM PUBLISHING**
75 Arlington Street, Boston, MA 02116
A Pearson Education Company

# TABLE OF CONTENTS

Preface

## PART I: WRITTEN COMMUNICATIONS

## PART IV: TECHNOLOGY

# PREFACE

As you continue on your pathway to success, your Skills Investment Portfolio (S.K.I.P.), is an important document and storage vehicle. It provides you with a record of the skills and knowledge that you have mastered and should help you to both visualize and achieve a path of continuous improvement.

Use the tabbed organization system provided in your Portfolio to organize your work. It is straightforward and easy to use and should help you locate information when you need it later. Your Portfolio should contain the following tabs:

PART I  ELEMENTS OF SUCCESS
        Motivators
        Mission
        Goals
        Systems That Work

PART II  INFORMATION PROCESSING
        Self Knowledge
        Learning (Style, Processing, and Retaining)
        Systems That Work

PART III  OVERCOMING OBSTACLES
        Resources
        Problem Solving Method
        Planning, Scheduling, and Time Management
        Systems That Work

PART IV  COMMUNICATION
        Written Skills
        Oral Skills
        Group Dynamics
        Leadership
        Systems That Work

PART V  SKILL IDENTIFICATION
        Self Assessment
        Transferable Skills
        Technical Skills
        Personal Traits

PART VI  CAREER DECISION-MAKING
        Values
        Employer Culture
        Personal Objectives
        Employment Decision-Making

PART VII  JOB SEARCH PROCESS
        Company Information
        Job Application
        Correspondence
        Resumes
        Interviewing
        Networking
        Negotiating Salary

The information that you file in S.K.I.P. will help you to prepare your final resume and prepare for job interviews, so it is important to file the materials from your Pathway to Success Forms Packet, Volume II in your Portfolio as you complete specific assignments.

Pathway to Success, Volume II is a workbook that contains Guidelines, Forms, and Assignments for Portfolio (Exercises intended to aid you in developing your critical thinking, communication, resource allocation, and technical skills.) Each of these items is intended to help you measure what you have achieved and to help you continuously improve your skills. In addition, by entering the forms in your Skills Investment Portfolio (S.K.I.P.), you will build a data bank of information that will:

1.  Facilitate your employment search;
2.  Help you to prepare a better resume; and
3.  Act as a reminder of the skills and content knowledge you need to master to maximize your employment opportunities.

The Guidelines are essentially checklists. They are deliberately brief and are intended as "reminders" as you seek to improve your skills in areas that are critical to your future success: trouble shooting (problem analysis and critical thinking), communication, and resource allocation. Each guideline includes information specifying where you should file it in your Portfolio.

The Forms require you to fill out information. They are intended to develop and reinforce skills and to record information that you will need to master or to use as you seek employment. Each form includes information specifying where you should file it in your Portfolio.

The Assignment for Portfolio materials are exercises. Generally, they provide information or a scenario and require you to complete a task. For example, an assignment may ask you to prepare a memo, a lab report or a specific type of resume. As with the Guidelines and the Forms, the Assignment for Portfolio is intended to develop and reinforce skills and to help you develop instruments, like a resume, that will enhance your job search efforts. Each Assignment for Portfolio includes information specifying where you should file it in your Portfolio.

Life is a journey and so are the skills that we acquire that help us to excel at it. Good luck to you as you continue your journey. Your success is in your hands! Apply yourself consistently and continuously strive to improve your skills, and it will pay dividends as you move forward along the path.

# PART I

# WRITTEN COMMUNICATIONS

**Paragraphs**
**Letters**
**Memos**
**Techniques for Reports**
**Types of Reports**
**Resume**

# WRITTEN COMMUNICATIONS

**FORM 1-1**
**See Part I of your Portfolio**

Revise Your Mission Statement

1.      Use the area below to outline the key points of your mission statement.

_____        _____

_____        _____

_____        _____

_____        _____

Mission Statement

_____

_____

_____

_____

_____

_____

_____

✔      Have you checked your work for spelling and grammar?

✔      Have you shared this with a fellow student to generate helpful feedback?

Insert Form in Part I, Mission, S.K.I.P.

Insert Form in Part I, Mission, S.K.I.P.

## Form 1-2
## Name and review goal analysis for Part I of your Portfolio

Name: _____         Date: _____

Prepare a paragraph describing/explaining your career objective(s).

Use the area below to outline your paragraph:

_____         _____

_____         _____

_____         _____

_____         _____

Career Objective Paragraph

_____

_____

_____

_____

✔    Have you checked your work for spelling and grammar?

✔    Have you shared this with a fellow student to generate helpful feedback?

Insert Form in Part I, Goals, S.K.I.P.

## Guideline 1-1
## General Letter Outline

---

_____ (inside address)

_____

_____ (date)

_____ (name)
_____ (title)
_____ (company)
_____ (address)

Dear _____: (name)

_____
_____
_____Introduction_____
_____
_____

_____
_____Discussion_____
_____
_____

_____
_____Conclusion_____
_____
_____

Sincerely,

_____ (your name in type)

cc:

---

Insert Guideline in Part IV, Written Skills, S.K.I.P.

## Guideline 1-2
## Writing Process A

☐    Prewriting

Following is a *reporters' questions checklist* for a letter of inquiry.

REPORTERS' QUESTIONS CHECKLIST

1.☐    Who is your audience?
    —Potential employer
    —High-tech peer
    —Low-tech peer
    —Lay reader
    —Management
    —Subordinate
    —Multiple audiences

2.☐    *Why* are you writing?

3.☐    *What* is the general topic of your request?

4.☐    *What* exactly do you want to know (the specifics itemized in the discussion paragraph of your letter?

5.☐    *What* do you want the reader to do next?

6.☐    *When* do you want the reader to act (dated action)?

7.☐    *Why* is this date important?

Insert Guideline in Part IV, Written Skills, S.K.I.P.

## Guideline 1-3
## Writing Process B

☐     Writing

✔     *Study the letter criteria.*

✔     *Review your prewriting.* Have you omitted any significant information? Have you included unnecessary information?

✔     *Organize the data for your discussion paragraph.* One organizational pattern especially effective for most letters is *importance.* When you organize by importance, you place the most important information first and the less important ideas later. To do so, you can use the inverted journalist's pyramid below.

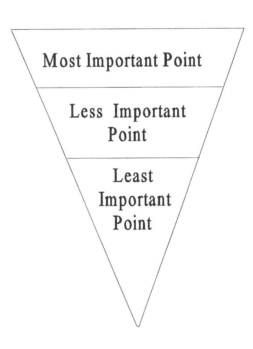

Most Important Point

Less Important Point

Least Important Point

**Guideline 1-4**
**Writing Process C**

As you rewrite, keep the following in mind:

✔ Clear

✔ Concise

✔ Appropriate to audience

✔ Logical structure

✔ Appropriate tone

✔ Error free

**Assignment for Portfolio 1-1**
**Letter to Potential Employer**
**Review Part I in your Portfolio**

Name:_____     Date: _____

Write a letter to potential employer requesting information, keep the following in mind:

1.      Location desired

2.      Type of work desired

3.      Type of firm

4.      Your qualifications


✔      Check Guidelines 1-1, 1-2, 1-3 and 1-4?

✔      Have you checked your work for spelling and grammar?

✔      Have you shared this with a fellow student to generate helpful feedback?

✔      Are you satisfied with this work?

✔      Place in Portfolio as a model of this type of letter.

Insert Assignment in Part VII, Correspondence, S.K.I.P.

## Assignment for Portfolio 1-2
## Cover Letter

Name:_____     Date: _____

Write a cover letter. Perhaps your cover letter will preface a lab report you're working on in school, a report you're writing at work, or documentation you'll need to send to a client. Use the criteria for writing cover letters and the writing process techniques found in Resource Digest.

✔ Remember: Cover letters inform readers about information that follows and focuses their attention on key points.

✔ Check Guidelines 1-1, 1-2, 1-3 and 1-4.

✔ Have you checked your work for spelling and grammar?

✔ Have you shared this with a fellow student to generate helpful feedback?

✔ Are you satisfied with this work?

✔ Place in your Portfolio as a model of this type of letter.

Insert Assignment in Part IV, Written Skills, S.K.I.P.

## Assignment for Portfolio 1-3
## Good News Letter

Name:_____          Date: _____

Write a good news letter. Commend a co-worker for a job well done. Congratulate a subordinate for his or her promotion. Better yet, write a thank-you letter to a teacher showing your appreciation for his or her professionalism and dedication. Follow the criteria for writing a good-news letter and the writing process techniques found in the Resource Digest.

✔     Check Guidelines 1-1, 1-2, 1-3 and 1-4.

✔     Have you checked your work for spelling and grammar?

✔     Have you shared this with a fellow student to generate helpful feedback?

✔     Are you satisfied with this work?

✔     Place in your Portfolio as a model of this type of letter.

## Assignment for Portfolio 1-4
## Collaborative Writing Exercise

Name:_____     Date: _____

After reading the following case studies, write the appropriate letters required for each assignment.

## Case Situations:

a.   Vivian Davis, who lives at 2939 Cactus, in Santa Clara, CA 95054, has invented a new product, VAST (a Voice Activated Speaker Telephone). This telephone can be "dialed" without the use of one's hands, simply by saying names or numbers into the systems speaker. Vivian believes that such a machine could benefit the handicapped, the elderly, the infirmed, homemakers, and business people. She can sell this phone for $25 to electronic stores, hobby shops, general-purpose retailers, etc., who then can market it for $50. Write a sales letter for Ms. Davis based on the preceding information.

b.   Mark Shabbot works for Apex, Inc., 1919 W. 23rd Street, Denver, CO 80204. Apex, a retailer of electronic equipment, wants to purchase 125 new oscilloscopes from a vendor, Omnico, located at 30467 Sheraton, Phoenix, AZ 85023. The oscilloscopes will be sold to a VO-Tech college in Denver (Northwest Hills Vocational-Technical College). However, before Apex purchases these oscilloscopes, Mark needs information regarding bulk rates, shipping schedules, maintenance agreements, equipment specifications, and machinery capabilities. Northwest Hills needs this equipment before the new term (August 15). Write a letter of inquiry for Mr. Shabbot based on the preceding information.

c.   Sharon Baker works as a technical writer for Prismatic Consulting Engineering, 123 Park, Boston, MA 01755. In response to an RFP (Request for Proposal), she has written a proposal to the Oceanview City Council, 457 E. Cypress Street, Oceanview, MA 01759. The proposal suggests ways in which Oceanview can improve its flood control. Now Sharon needs to write a cover letter prefacing her proposal. In this cover letter, she wants to call her readers' attention to key concerns within the proposal; suggested costs, time frames, potential problems which could occur if the proposed suggestions are not implemented, ways in which the proposal will solve the problems, and Prismatic's credentials. Once the Oceanview City Council receives the proposal, Prismatic representatives will contact them for follow-up discussions. Write Ms. Baker's cover letter based on the preceding information.

Insert Assignment in Part IV, Written Skills, S.K.I.P.

## CASE SITUATIONS (Continued)

d.  Bob Ward, a lineworker at HomeCare Health Equipment, 8025 Industrial Parkway, Ashley, NC 27709, deserves a letter of commendation for his excellent job record. He has not missed a day of work in five years. In addition, his production line has achieved a 5% error reading (7% considered acceptable). He has also trained new hires.  Most importantly, he made six suggestions for improvements, three of which saved the company money. The company president, Peter Tsui, based at Home Care's home office at 4791 Research Avenue, Wasa, MN 55900, wants to award Bob with a plaque at the annual awards dinner, September 7, 1992. Write Mr. Tsui's good-news letter based on the preceding information.

e.  Craig Salvay works as a service technician for EEE Electronics Servicing, 11201 Blanco, Santa Fe, NM 88004.  Yesterday, he went to Schoss-McGraw Associates, 1628 W. 18th Street, Taos, NM 88003, to service their computer systems. He billed them $75 for his time, but he did not bill them for parts since the machinery was supposedly under warranty. However, when he returned to EEE, Craig's manager, Marilyn Hoover, informed Craig that the machinery was not under warranty and that Schoss-McGraw would have to be billed an additional $45.87 for parts. Schoss-McGraw is an excellent client, so Marilyn wants Craig to be especially tactful in requesting the additional money.  Based on the preceding information, write Craig's bad-news letter.


✔  Have you checked your work for spelling and grammar?

✔  Have you shared this with a fellow student to generate helpful feedback?

✔  Are you satisfied with this work?

✔  Place in your Portfolio as a model of this type of letter.

Insert Assignment in Part IV, Written Skills, S.K.I.P.

**Form 1-3**
**Systems That Work**

Name:_____     Date: _____


## Letter Guidelines That Work For You

Rate the techniques or skills that helped you most to write these letters. 1 is low and 5 is high:

|  | 1 | 2 | 3 | 4 | 5 |
|---|---|---|---|---|---|
| 1. Clarify Intent<br>    Did you complete the following?<br>        Audience analysis<br>        Purpose analysis |  |  |  |  |  |
| 2. Formulate Discussion<br>    Did you gather information and data? |  |  |  |  |  |
| 3. Precise Close |  |  |  |  |  |
| 4. Peer Review/Collaborative |  |  |  |  |  |
| 5. Create Mail-Ready Copy<br>    Did you:<br>      *Edit and rewrite?<br>      *Proof? |  |  |  |  |  |

*Note that different letters use different techniques or skills.

## Guideline 1-5
## Memos Versus Letters

**Memos**
- ☐ Internal correspondence (written within your company to one of your colleagues

- ☐ Memo format (Date, To, From, Subject)

- ☐ Generally high-tech audience (peers)

- ☐ High-tech subject matter with abbreviations and acronyms often allowed

- ☐ Informal tone (due to peer audience)

**Letters**
- ☐ External correspondence (written outside your business to a vendor or client, for example)

- ☐ Letter format (Letterhead Address, Inside Address, Salutation, Complimentary Close)

- ☐ Generally low-tech or lay audience

- ☐ Low-tech/layperson's subject matter with abbreviations and acronyms defined clearly

- ☐ More formal tone (due to audience with whom you may not be familiar)

**Guideline 1-6**
**Memo Outline**

DATE:

TO:

FROM:

SUBJECT:    | Focus + Topic? |

| Introduction: | A lead-in, warm-up, overview stating *why* you're writing and *what* you're writing about. |

| Discussion: | Detailed development, made accessible through highlighting techniques, explaining *exactly what* you want to say. |

| Conclusion: | A summation stating *what's next, when* this will occur, and *why* the date is important. |

## Assignment for Portfolio 1-5
## Create a Memo

Prepare a memo based on the following case:

> Bob Ward, a lineworker at HomeCare Health Equipment, 8025 Industrial Parkway, Ashley, NC 27709, deserves a letter of commendation for his excellent job record. He has not missed a day of work in five years. In addition, his production line has achieved a 5% error reading (7% considered acceptable). He has also trained new hires. Most importantly, he made six suggestions for improvements, three of which saved the company money. His manager, Peter Tsui, has been asked to write a memo recommending him for an award.

✔ Remember to focus on subject line.

✔ Remember to provide overview in the introduction.

✔ Remember to answer key fact questions: who, what, where, when, why, and how.

✔ Remember to have clear purpose in close.

✔ Have you checked your spelling?

✔ Are you satisfied with this work?

✔ Place in your Portfolio as a model of this type of memo.

Insert Assignment in Part IV, Written Skills, S.K.I.P.

## Assignment for Portfolio 1-6
## Memos/Collaborative Writing

Each student will write the memo requested by the instructor. To do so, first prewrite (using mind mapping/clustering), then write a draft and finally rewrite (revising your draft).

Once the memos are written, evaluate them in your peer review group. Decide which memos are successful (how and why) and which memos need revision. In the peer group revise the flawed memos. Consider the criteria for good memos and the rewriting techniques presented. Make up any details considered necessary to improve the memo. Each group will turn in one corrected memo for evaluation.

## EXERCISE

1.  Your work environment is experiencing a problem (with scheduling, layoffs, turnover, production, quality, morale, etc.). Your boss has asked you to write a memo noting the problem and suggesting solutions.

2.  An employee under your supervision sees a problem in his or her work environment and has written a memo suggesting a solution. You don't believe the suggested solution will work. Write a memo providing your response.

3.  A major project is being introduced at work. Write a directive memo informing your work team of their individual responsibilities and schedules.

4.  Your department needs a new piece of equipment to perform work. Write a memo requesting this equipment. Justify the need for the equipment and give the date when the equipment is needed.

5.  You work in the purchasing department and must buy a new piece of equipment. You must first compare bids. You've done so and now must write a comparison/contrast memo explaining why you plan to purchase one piece of equipment versus another.

6.  It's time for your quality circle team (or any committee you chair) to meet again. Write a memo calling the meeting. Provide an agenda.

## Form 1-4
## Rating Your Memos

Rate your memos. 1 is low and 5 is high:

| MEMO RATING FORM | 1 | 2 | 3 | 4 | 5 |
|---|---|---|---|---|---|
| 1. Focused Subject Line | | | | | |
| 2. Introduction Provides Overview | | | | | |
| 3. Discussion | | | | | |
| *Who | | | | | |
| *What | | | | | |
| *Why | | | | | |
| *When | | | | | |
| *Where | | | | | |
| *How | | | | | |
| 4. Conclusion -- <br> Provide recommendation and/or ask for action | | | | | |

## Form 1-5
## Writing Definitions

Rate your skill in writing definitions. 1 is low and 5 is high:

| GUIDELINES FOR WRITING DEFINITIONS | 1 | 2 | 3 | 4 | 5 |
|---|---|---|---|---|---|
| ✔ Keep it simple | | | | | |
| ✔ Use informal definitions for simple terms most readers understand | | | | | |
| ✔ Use formal definitions for more complex terms | | | | | |
| ✔ Use expanded definitions for supporting information | | | | | |
| ✔ Choose the right location for your definition | | | | | |

Insert Form in Part IV, Systems That Work, S.K.I.P.

Insert Form in Part IV, Systems That Work, S.K.I.P.

## Form 1-6
## Sample Technical Description

Use this form as a checklist to rate the technical descriptions you are preparing. 1 is low and 5 is high:

| EFFECTIVE TECHNICAL DESCRIPTIONS INCLUDE: | 1 | 2 | 3 | 4 | 5 |
|---|---|---|---|---|---|
| ✔ A title | | | | | |
| ✔ An excellent introduction that lists topic, function, and components | | | | | |
| ✔ An effectively drawn and placed graph | | | | | |
| ✔ A reader-friendly discussion with headings exactly corresponding to the call-outs in the drawing | | | | | |
| ✔ A precisely detailed discussion focusing on materials, color, dimensions, etc. | | | | | |
| ✔ An effective conclusion | | | | | |

## Form 1-7
## Effective Instruction Checklist

Are you writing instructions effectively? Use the following as a checklist or to rate your style. 1 is low and 5 is high:

| EFFECTIVE INSTRUCTION CHECKLIST | 1 | 2 | 3 | 4 | 5 |
|---|---|---|---|---|---|
| Use the following checklist to make sure that your instruction is effectively written. | | | | | |
| ✔ *Does the instruction have an effective introduction?* | | | | | |
| —Is the topic mentioned? | | | | | |
| —Are the steps listed? | | | | | |
| —Has a reason for performing the operation been provided? | | | | | |
| —Are ease of use or capabilities mentioned? | | | | | |
| —Has a list of required tools been provided? | | | | | |
| ✔ *Are the steps in the instruction's discussion effectively developed?* | | | | | |
| —Will a low-tech or lay reader be able to perform the requested operations based on what has been said, or must additional information be added for clarity? | | | | | |
| ✔ *Is the instruction's discussion effectively presented?* | | | | | |
| —Are the steps overloaded and difficult to follow, or does each step present one clearly defined operation? | | | | | |
| —Are highlighting techniques effectively used? These should include graphics such as comic-book-look photographs or line drawings and correctly placed emphatic warnings (using color and/or universal symbols). | | | | | |

**Form 1-7 (Continued)**

| | | | | | |
|---|---|---|---|---|---|
| ✔ *Does the instruction's discussion contain the same number of steps as mentioned in the introduction?* | | | | | |
| ✔ *Is the discussion organized chronologically?* | | | | | |
| ✔ *Do the steps begin with verbs?* | | | | | |
| ✔ *Does the instruction reveal a correct sense of audience?* | | | | | |
| —High tech? | | | | | |
| —Low tech? | | | | | |
| —Lay readers? | | | | | |
| —Sexist language avoided? | | | | | |
| —Personalized words (pronouns) used? | | | | | |
| ✔ *Is the conclusion effective?* | | | | | |
| —Have warranties been mentioned? | | | | | |
| —Is a sales pitch provided showing the ease of use? | | | | | |
| —Has the conclusion reiterated a reason for performing the steps? | | | | | |
| —Does the conclusion focus on credentials? | | | | | |
| —Are disclaimers provided? | | | | | |
| ✔ *Is correct technical writing style used?* | | | | | |
| ✔ *Have grammatical and textual errors been avoided?* | | | | | |

Insert Form in Part IV, Systems That Work, S.K.I.P.

## Guideline 1-7
## Structure of a Laboratory Report

A laboratory report comprises several readily identifiable compartments, each usually preceded by a heading. These compartments are described briefly here:

| Part | Section Title | Contents |
|------|---------------|----------|
| SUMMARY | **Summary** | A very brief statement of the purpose of the tests, the main findings, and what can be interpreted from them. (In short laboratory reports, the summary can be combined with the next compartment.) |
| BACKGROUND | **Objective** | A more detailed description of why the tests were performed, on whose authority they were conducted, and what they were expected to achieve or prove. |
| FACTS | | *There are four parts here:* |
| | **Equipment** | A description of the test setup, plus a list of equipment and materials used. A drawing of the test hook-up may be inserted here. (If a series of tests is being performed, with a different equipment setup for each test, then a separate equipment description, materials list, and illustration should be inserted immediately before each test description.) |
| | **Test Method** | A detailed, step-by-step explanation of the tests. In industrial laboratory reports the depth of explanation depends on the reader's needs: if a reader is nontechnical and likely to be interested only in results, then the test description can be condensed. For lab reports written at a college or university, however, students are expected to provide a thorough description here. |
| | **Test Results** | Usually a brief statement of the test results or the findings evolving from the tests. |

Insert Guideline in Part IV, Written Skills, S.K.I.P.

**Guideline 1-7 (Continued)**

|  | **Analysis (or Interpretation** | A detailed discussion of the results or findings, their implications, and what can be interpreted from them. (The analysis section is particularly important in academic lab reports.) |
| OUTCOME | **Conclusions** | A brief summing-up which shows how the test results, findings, and analysis meet the objective(s) established at the start of the report. |
| BACKUP | **Attachments** | These are pages of supporting data such as test measurements derived during the tests, or documentation such as specifications, procedures, instructions, and drawings, which would interrupt reading continuity if placed in the report narrative (in the test method section). |

## Guideline 1-8
## Short Report Criteria Checklist

Use the following short-report criteria checklist to help you in writing your short report.

✔  *Does your subject line contain a topic and a focus?* If you write only "Subject: Trip Report" or "Subject: Feasibility Report," you have not communicated thoroughly to your reader. Such a subject line merely presents the focus of your correspondence. But what's the topic? To provide both topic and focus, you need to write "Subject: Trip Report on Solvent Training Course, Arco Corporation -- 3/15/91" or "Subject: Feasibility Report on Company Expansion to Bolker Blvd."

✔  *Does the introduction explain the purpose of the report, document the personnel involved, and/or state when and where the activities occurred?*

✔  *When you write the discussion section of the report, do you quantify what occurred?* In this section, you must clarify precisely. Supply accurate dates, times, calculations, and problems encountered.

✔  *Is the discussion accessible?* To create reader-friendly ease of access, use highlighting techniques, such as headings, boldface, underlining, and itemization. You also might want to use graphics, such as pie charts, bar charts, or tables.

✔  *Have you selected an appropriate method of organization in your discussion?* You can use chronology, importance, comparison/contrast, and/or problem/solution to document your findings.

✔  *Does your conclusion present a value judgment regarding the findings presented in the discussion?* The discussion states the facts; the conclusion decides what these facts mean.

✔  *In your recommendations, do you tell your reader(s) what to do next or what you consider to be the appropriate course of action?*

✔  *Have you maintained a low fog index for readability?*

✔  *Have you effectively recognized your audience's level of understanding (high tech, low tech, lay, management, subordinate, colleague) and written accordingly?*

✔  *Is your report accurate?* Correct grammar and calculations make a difference. If you've made errors in spelling, punctuation, grammar, or mathematics, you will look unprofessional.

## Guideline 1-9
## Long Reports and Proposals

Since short reports run only a few pages, you can assume that your readers will be able to follow your train of thought easily. Thus, short reports merely require that you use headings such as "Introduction," "Discussion," and "Conclusion/Recommendation" to guide your readers through the correspondence.

Long reports, however, place a greater demand on readers. Your audience will be overwhelmed with numerous pages of information. A few headings won't be enough to help your readers wade through the data. To guide your readers through a proposal, you'll need to provide the following:

☐    Cover letter

☐    Title page

☐    Table of contents

☐    List of illustrations

☐    Abstract (or executive summary)

☐    Introduction

☐    Discussion (the body of the long report)

☐    Conclusion/Recommendation

☐    Glossary

☐    Works Cited page (if you're documenting research; this is discussed in Chapter 5)

☐    Appendix

---

Insert Guideline in Part IV, Written Skills, S.K.I.P.

## Guideline 1-10
## Cover Letter for Long Report

Your cover letter prefaces the long report and provides the reader an overview of what is to follow. It tells the reader:

- ☐ Why you are writing

- ☐ What you are writing about (the subject of this report)

- ☐ What exactly of importance is within the report

- ☐ What you plan to do next as a follow-up

- ☐ When the action should occur

## Guideline 1-11
## Article Review

I.  IDENTIFICATION OF ARTICLE

    A.    Subject

    B.    Article title

    C.    Author (if listed)

    D.    Magazine title

    E.    Date of magazine

    F.    Page number(s)

II.  SUMMARY OF ARTICLE

    A.    Author's main point(s) or purpose

    B.    Supporting examples or data

    C.    Author bias

III.  APPLICATION TO LIFE

(How does the article apply to life, goals, or specific challenges of the student or member of the family?)

IV.  STUDENT OPINION

    A.    Agreement/disagreement with author's point of view (Do you agree or disagree with the author?)

    B.    Support of opinion. (Defend your opinion.)

    C.    Recommendation of article. (Would you recommend this article and why?)

Insert Guideline in Part IV, Systems That Work, S.K.I.P.

# DISC RESUME FOR WINDOWS

# STUDENT MANUAL

## TABLE OF CONTENTS

*Welcome to Disc Resume for Windows!*

*Let's get started....*

Opening Disc Resume for Windows:

    With Windows 3.x or Windows NT 3.x:
- Choose File>Run
- Run A:\Resume96.exe (or B:\Resume96.exe)

    With Windows 95 or Windows NT 4.0:
- Choose Start>Run
- Run A:\Resume96.exe (or B:\Resume96.exe)

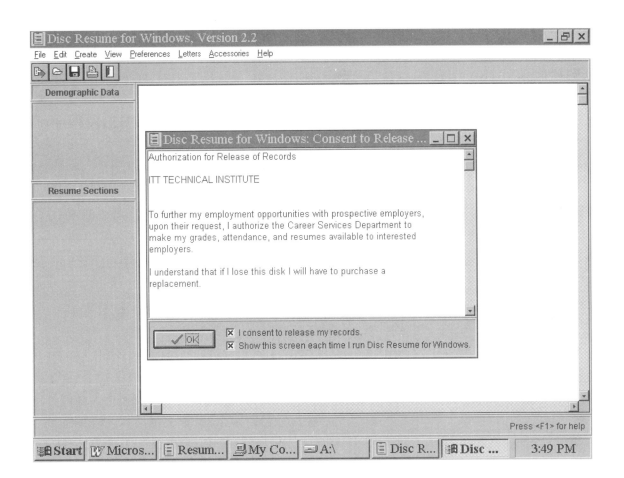

Once the Disc Resume for Windows is successfully opened, a **Consent to Release Records** screen will appear. Please check the box stating "I consent to release my records." This will give the Career Services Department the ability to fully assist you in your job search by allowing your academic history to be available to a prospective employer if requested.

Once you have completed this section, click *O.K.*

Now you are ready to begin building your resume!

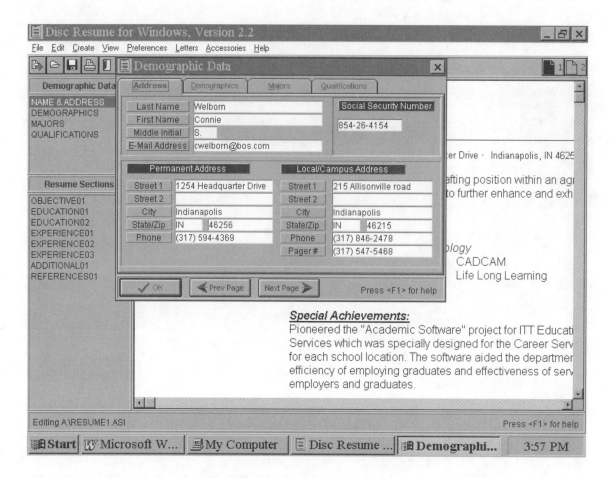

You will then see the main menu for Disc Resume for Windows. Each field located on the left portion of the screen is to help you format the information in your resume and is also used by the Director of Career Services as a guide in assisting you with your employment search.

**DEMOGRAPHIC DATA:**

***NAME & ADDRESS***

To open the first demographic field, double click on ***NAME & ADDRESS.***

- Enter the appropriate information. Keep in mind this information will be reflected on your resume exactly how it is entered (all caps, lowercase, etc.).

- It is not necessary to enter both a permanent and local address.

    Once you have completed this section, click ***O.K.***

44

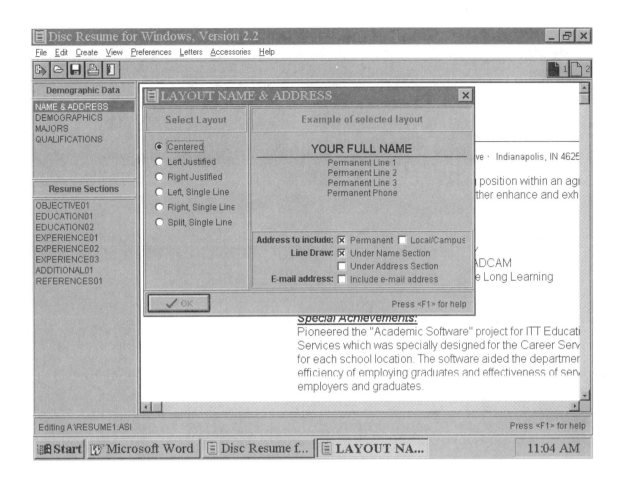

To change the layout of your name and address, highlight the **NAME &
ADDRESS** field to the left of your screen and right mouse click. If you choose
the option *LAYOUT NAME & ADDRESS*, you will have the ability to manipulate
how the information will appear. This screen also allows you to determine
exactly which portion of this section will appear (i.e. email address, local address,
etc.)

Once you have completed this section, click **O.K.**

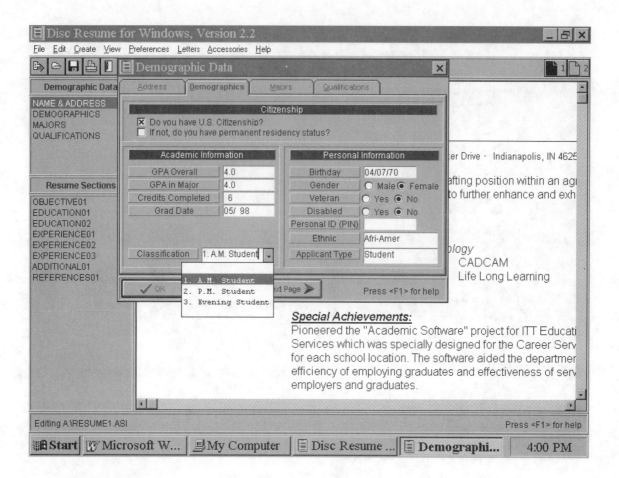

## DEMOGRAPHICS

To open the next section entitled **DEMOGRAPHICS,** double click on *DEMOGRAPHICS* listed at the left side of your screen

- The information obtained in this section is for the Director of Career Services use only. This information will not appear on your resume. The data collected from this portion is used to better service you in your employment search.

- The *CLASSIFICATION, ETHNIC*, and *APPLICANT TYPE* fields each have a drop down box which is accessed by simply clicking anywhere in the box.

Once you have completed this section, click **O.K.**

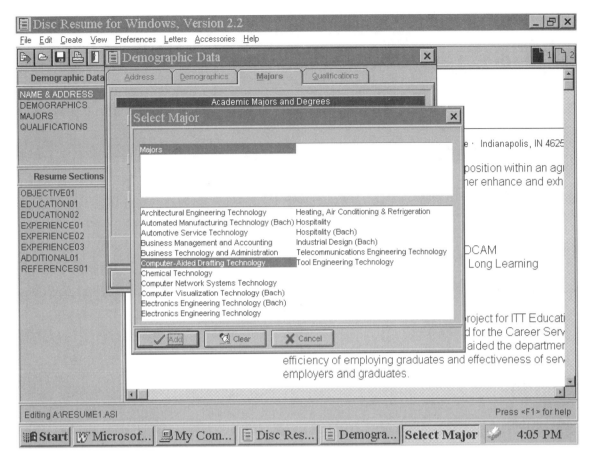

## MAJORS

The next portion of the demographic data, **MAJORS**, can be accessed by double clicking on the *MAJORS* field located at the left of your screen.

- The information obtained in this section is for the Director of Career Services use only. This information will not appear on your resume. The data collected from this portion is used to better service your employment search.

- To select your current major, simply click on the arrow located at the end of the field and a drop down box will appear.

- To select the degree sought, click inside the *DEGREE* field, and a drop down screen will once again appear.

- You may use the *MAJOR 2* and *MAJOR 3* fields to add any additional degrees you may have already obtained.

  Once you have completed this section, click **O.K.**

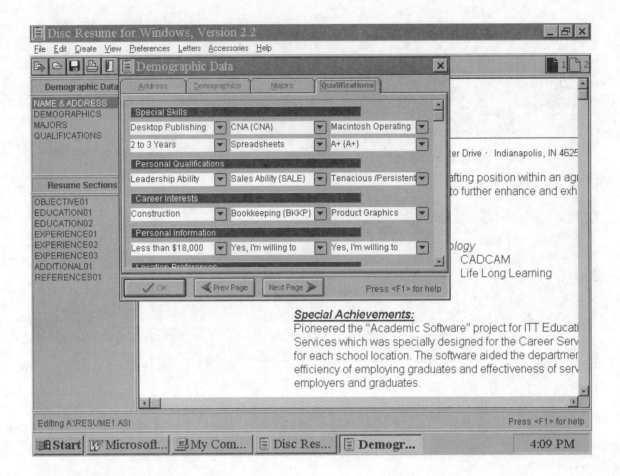

## QUALIFICATIONS

Open the last section of the *DEMOGRAPHIC DATA* by double clicking on **QUALIFICATIONS** to the left of your screen.

- Once again the information obtained in the *QUALIFICATIONS* portion will not appear on your resume. The Director of Career Services will use this information to screen employment opportunities for you.

- Each subcategory within this section allows you six choices. Simply click on the down arrow in each field and a drop down box will appear.

  Once you have completed this section, click **O.K.**

We have now finished our demographic data. Keep in mind the only portion of your resume we have completed is your name and address. Let's move to the **RESUME SECTIONS** category and get to the meat of your resume!

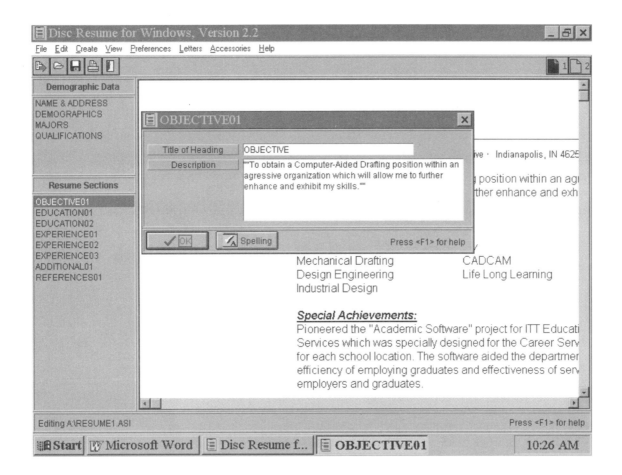

\*The following information will be included on your resume.

## RESUME SECTIONS

### OBJECTIVE

To begin the body of your resume, double click on the **OBJECTIVE** section. Be aware that your information will appear exactly how it is entered (caps, lower case, etc.)

- The **TITLE OF HEADING** gives you the ability to name the field (i.e. Objective, Career Goals, etc.)

- Be sure to utilize the spell check function.

  Once you have completed this section, click **O.K.**

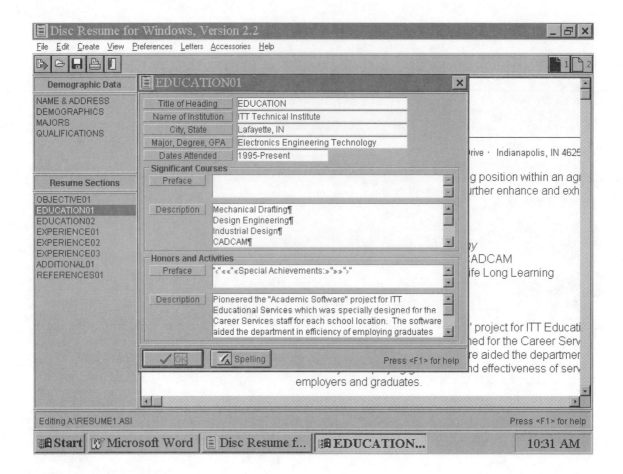

## EDUCATION

Once the *OBJECTIVE* section of your resume is completed, you are now ready to move to your educational background. Open the **EDUCATION** portion of your resume by double clicking on the **EDUCATION** field to the left of the screen.

- The **TITLE OF HEADING** section once again gives you the opportunity to name this section (i.e. Educational Background, Academic History, etc.).

- Input the appropriate information in the following boxes.

- The **SIGNIFICANT COURSES** portion is asking for the title of the courses you have taken or will be taking. The description box is asking for a course description.

- The **HONORS AND ACTIVITIES** section is asking for any honors you have achieved or activities you have been a part of which will be a favorable reflection for you with an employer.

  Once you have completed this section, click **O.K.**

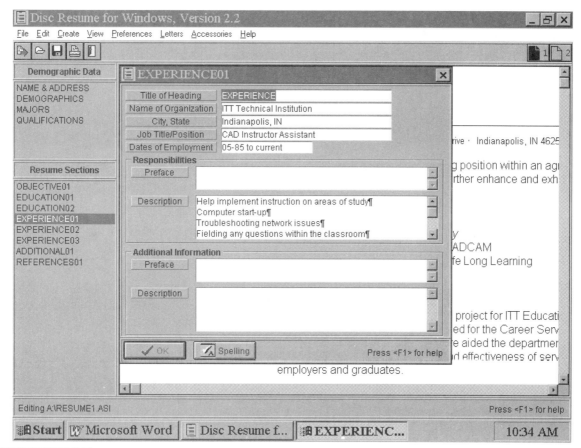

## EXPERIENCE

You are now ready to advance to the **EXPERIENCE** section of your resume. Once again, you may open this field by double clicking on **EXPERIENCE** to the left of your screen.

- The **TITLE OF HEADING** again gives you the option of naming this portion of your resume (i.e. Employment History, Work Experience, etc.).

- Fill in the following information appropriately.

- The **PREFACE** section is optional. This would be useful for if you plan to list a group of responsibilities in the *DESCRIPTION* portion (i.e. the *PREFACE* section would read, "Responsibilities included:", and the *DESCRIPTION* section would contain a list of your duties.)

- **ADDITIONAL INFORMATION** functions similarly to the *HONORS AND ACTIVITIES* fields of the previously mentioned *EDUCATION* section.

    Once you have completed this section, click **O.K.**

51

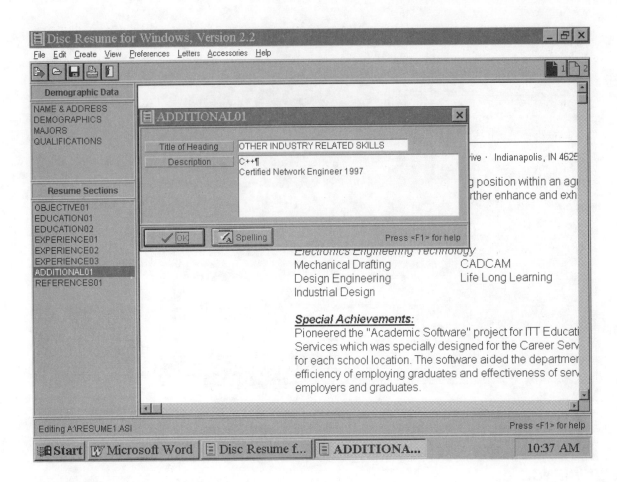

## ADDITIONAL

The **ADDITIONAL** section can serve many functions. This section can be utilized to list any additional industry-related skills you may possess or used to notate any special certificates or certifications you may have acquired or are working towards. You may name this section by entering your heading the *TITLE OF HEADING* section.

Once you have completed this section, click **O.K.**

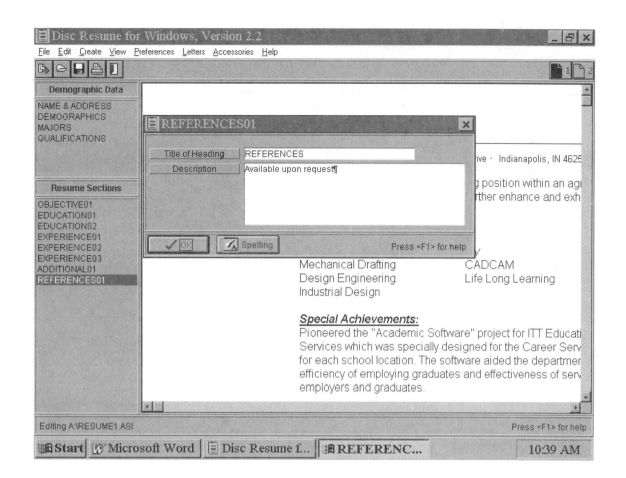

Enter the action you wish the employer to take to obtain your references (i.e. "Available Upon Request").

Once you have completed this section, click **O.K.**

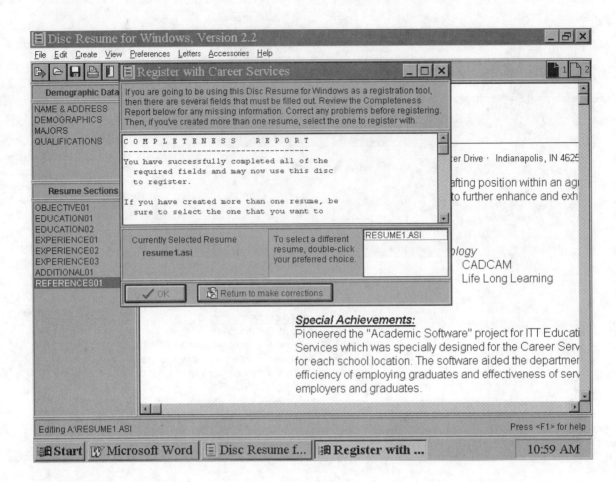

Once all information is entered to your liking, you may now exit the Resume Disc by choosing *FILE>EXIT*.

If each field has been entered correctly, a **COMPLETENESS REPORT** will be displayed reflecting such. If in fact corrections need to be made or you wish to change the layout of your resume, simply click on *RETURN TO MAKE CORRECTIONS*.

*Notice: If you have created two resumes on this disc, please notate which resume you wish to be printed on this screen.*

YOUR RESUME IS NOW COMPLETE!

CONGRATULATIONS!

# CHANGING FORMAT/LAYOUT

To change the layout of your resume or any section within the resume, simply highlight the section title from the left portion of the screen, right mouse click, and choose from the following:

**Edit Section**: By selecting Edit Section, you are given the opportunity to change any information you have entered. If you would like any information **bolded**, underlined, or *italicized*, highlight the word or section and right mouse click.

**Delete Section**: By selecting Delete Section, you can delete any section in which you have two or more entries.

**Move Section**: You have the ability to change the order in which the sections appear on your resume by selecting the Move Section option.

**Create Section**: By selecting Create Section, you can have multiple sections under the same category (i.e. Education01, Education02, etc).

**Layout Section**: By highlighting this option, you will be given three tabs which give you the capability of changing the format and look of your resume:

First Tab: Here you are given the ability to change the look of the section (i.e. left full, left indented, paragraph form, etc.) You are also given the choice of **not printing** a particular section. If you are customizing a resume, this option may be helpful. **Compressing** a section is done within this tab, too. This function can help reduce the overall size of the resume.

Second Tab: **Bulleting, lists**, and **columns** can be formatted in this tab.

Third Tab: **Bulleting, lists,** and **columns** can be formatted in this tab for any information contained in the ADDITIONAL fields.

* By clicking on PREFERENCES located within the tool bar, you may change the overall **format** and **font** style of your resume.

* You may create **multiple resumes** on this disc. Select FILE>CREATE from your tool bar.

* Each of the previous functions can be performed also by utilizing EDIT and CREATE found within the tool bar.

55

## Introduction
## Resume Writing

Like any writing assignment, the writing process depends upon the quality of the information with which you start.  If you carefully assemble your facts before you start to write, the process is both easier and more effective and the end result is a better demonstration of the skills that you bring to the task.

The following will help you gather the data you will need to prepare an effective resume and will also give you the information you need to defend or elaborate upon your resume in an interview.

Before we proceed, let's review the information you generated in Quarter 1.  You should review information in Part 1, 5 and 6 or your Portfolio.

It's now been several months since you worked on these forms and it's now time to update the information.

**Form 1-8**
**Transferable Skills**

Name:_____       Date: _____

### *What are transferable skills and*
### *How to they affect your future?*

Many of the skills that you possess can be transferred from one job to another. For instance, word processing is a skill that can be used in a variety of jobs. Skills, such as the ability to effectively communicate your ideas, solve problems, make decisions, lead a team, can all be used in most working environments. In this section you will be spending time defining your skills list and then categorizing them into skills that can be transferred into the work force. The benefit to you is that the next time you apply for a job, you will be able to communicate to your future employer how you will be able to contribute to the company.

There are two ways to look at your skills. First, skills are activities that you can do. Second, however, is the fact that skills can be the style or method by which you do activities. For instance, you may have word processing skills. That skill is an activity skill. But what are your skills as a word processor -- what style or method to you use? Maybe you are an accurate word processor. Perhaps you're fast. You can then state the skills you possess are "quickness" and "accuracy."

Look over the following list of skills and place a 1-4 in the space provided. Use the chart that begins on the next page to decide how much mastery you have gained in each skill.

> 1 = Have not developed
> 2 = Needs more practice
> 3 = Have some competency
> 4 = Have a satisfactory degree of mastery

Add skills rated 4 to your Disc Resume for Windows.

---

Insert Form in Part V, Transferable Skills, S.K.I.P.

| TIME MANAGEMENT SKILLS | ANSWER HERE | | | |
|---|---|---|---|---|
| CAN YOU: | 1 | 2 | 3 | 4 |
| Identify tasks to be completed? | | | | |
| Rank tasks by their importance? | | | | |
| Construct a time-line? | | | | |
| *Estimate* task *priorities* such as: | | | | |
| Time needed to complete | | | | |
| Time available | | | | |
| Levels of importance | | | | |
| Develop and follow schedules? | | | | |
| Avoid wasting time? | | | | |
| Evaluate and adjust a schedule? | | | | |

| PROBLEM-SOLVING SKILLS | ANSWER IIERE | | | |
|---|---|---|---|---|
| CAN YOU: | 1 | 2 | 3 | 4 |
| Think creatively? | | | | |
| Come up with new ideas? | | | | |
| Brainstorm with others? | | | | |
| Focus on details? | | | | |
| Listen to new ideas? | | | | |
| Research the opposition and history of a conflict? | | | | |
| Set realistic and attainable goals? | | | | |
| Present arguments objectively? | | | | |
| Listen to, hear and reflect on what's been said? | | | | |
| *Try to determine* what each party's *bottom line* is? | | | | |

Insert Form in Part V, Transferable Skills, S.K.I.P.

1=Have not developed    2=Needs more practice   3=Have some competency   4=Have a satisfactory degree of mastery

| PROBLEM-SOLVING SKILLS (CONTINUED) | ANSWER HERE | | | |
|---|---|---|---|---|
| CAN YOU: | 1 | 2 | 3 | 4 |
| Clarify problems? | | | | |
| Adjust quickly to new ideas and facts? | | | | |
| Propose and examine possible options? | | | | |
| Make reasonable compromises? | | | | |

| TEAM WORK SKILLS | ANSWER HERE | | | |
|---|---|---|---|---|
| CAN YOU: | 1 | 2 | 3 | 4 |
| Delegate responsibility of tasks to team members? | | | | |
| Work cooperatively with others? | | | | |
| Share tasks with others on the team? | | | | |
| Address and solve conflicts? | | | | |
| Recognize and build other's strengths? | | | | |
| Resolve differences for the sake of the group? | | | | |
| Take responsibility to accomplish the goals set by your team? | | | | |

| MATHEMATICAL SKILLS | ANSWER HERE | | | |
|---|---|---|---|---|
| CAN YOU: | 1 | 2 | 3 | 4 |
| Add? | | | | |
| Subtract? | | | | |
| Divide? | | | | |
| Multiply? | | | | |
| Do fractions? | | | | |
| Do story problems? | | | | |
| Figure out sales tax? | | | | |

Insert Form in Part V, Transferable Skills, S.K.I.P.

## Form 1-8 (Continued)

1=Have not developed    2=Needs more practice   3=Have some competency    4=Have a satisfactory degree of mastery

| MATHEMATICAL SKILLS (CONTINUED) | ANSWER HERE | | | |
|---|---|---|---|---|
| **CAN YOU:** | 1 | 2 | 3 | 4 |
| Split a check in a restaurant? | | | | |
| Balance a check book? | | | | |
| Calculate bargains? | | | | |
| Use a budget? | | | | |
| Project costs and revenues? | | | | |
| Calculate *budget needs?* | | | | |
| Figure out if actual costs and revenues differ from the estimated budget? | | | | |

| WRITTEN COMMUNICATION SKILLS | ANSWER HERE | | | |
|---|---|---|---|---|
| **CAN YOU:** | 1 | 2 | 3 | 4 |
| Punctuate correctly? | | | | |
| Write full sentences? | | | | |
| Avoid run-on sentences? | | | | |
| Use topic sentences in a paragraph? | | | | |
| Write creatively? | | | | |
| Write quickly? | | | | |
| Write a business letter? | | | | |
| Summarize an article? | | | | |
| Write a memo? | | | | |
| Complete a lab report? | | | | |
| Write a short report? | | | | |
| Write a long report? | | | | |
| Write a proposal? | | | | |

Insert Form in Part V, Transferable Skills, S.K.I.P.

1=Have not developed    2=Needs more practice   3=Have some competency    4=Have a satisfactory degree of mastery

| TECHNOLOGICAL SKILLS | ANSWER HERE | | | |
|---|---|---|---|---|
| CAN YOU: | 1 | 2 | 3 | 4 |
| Use data and other information by entering it into the computer? | | | | |
| Choose the best format for displays? | | | | |
| Line graphs? | | | | |
| Bar graphs? | | | | |
| Pie charts? | | | | |
| Write technical descriptions? | | | | |
| Write technical instructions? | | | | |
| Write technical definitions? | | | | |
| Write software (used in your program of study)? | | | | |
| Read and follow instructions for technical repair? | | | | |

| ORAL COMMUNICATION SKILLS | ANSWER HERE | | | |
|---|---|---|---|---|
| CAN YOU: | 1 | 2 | 3 | 4 |
| Talk to your supervisor with confidence? | | | | |
| Explain problems effectively? | | | | |
| Exchange information clearly? | | | | |
| Speak comfortably in small groups? | | | | |
| Speak comfortably in large groups? | | | | |
| Decide which information is important to be communicated? | | | | |
| Listen actively to identify needs and avoid misunderstandings? | | | | |
| Stay calm even when you're upset or angry? | | | | |

Insert Form in Part V, Transferable Skills, S.K.I.P.

## Form 1-8 (Continued)

1=Have not developed    2=Needs more practice   3=Have some competency    4=Have a satisfactory degree of mastery

| TYPING/COMPUTER | ANSWER HERE | | | |
|---|---|---|---|---|
| CAN YOU: | 1 | 2 | 3 | 4 |
| Type accurately? | | | | |
| Type correctly? | | | | |
| Make graphs? | | | | |
| Develop spread sheets? | | | | |
| Use spread sheets? | | | | |
| Use word processing? | | | | |
|    Use macro commands? | | | | |
|    Move text within a document? | | | | |
|    Spell check? | | | | |
|    Generate a table of contents? | | | | |
|    Print envelopes? | | | | |
|    Mail merge? | | | | |
| Create presentation graphics? | | | | |
| Manage a database? | | | | |
| Utilize project management software? | | | | |
| Use other software? | | | | |
| List: _____ | | | | |
|    _____ | | | | |

Insert Form in Part V, Transferable Skills, S.K.I.P.

**Form 1-8 (Continued)**

1=Have not developed    2=Needs more practice    3=Have some competency    4=Have a satisfactory degree of mastery

| ADMINISTRATIVE SKILLS | ANSWER HERE | | | |
|---|---|---|---|---|
| CAN YOU: | 1 | 2 | 3 | 4 |
| Answer telephones politely? | | | | |
| Manage more than one phone line at a time? | | | | |
| Copy large volumes of paper? | | | | |
| Collate and organize many copies of the same document? | | | | |
| Use a filing system? | | | | |
| Create a filing system? | | | | |
| Develop a plan on how to staff people? | | | | |
| Supervise others? | | | | |

| RESEARCH SKILLS | ANSWER HERE | | | |
|---|---|---|---|---|
| CAN YOU: | 1 | 2 | 3 | 4 |
| Collect information from various sources? | | | | |
| Analyze questions to determine what information is needed? | | | | |
| Select information most helpful to solving the problem? | | | | |
| Evaluate the information? | | | | |
| Use a card catalog? | | | | |
| Use a computer to conduct word searches? | | | | |
| Use Internet? | | | | |

Insert Form in Part V, Transferable Skills, S.K.I.P.

Insert Form in Part V, Transferable Skills, S.K.I.P.

**Form 1-9**
**SCANS Related Objectives**
See Pages 330-332 in WRITTEN COMMUNICATIONS RESOURCE DIGEST for additional detail.

Name:_____     Date:_____

Rate the following skills between 1 and 5 in accordance to the importance for our graduates.
1 = no importance and 5 = extremely important

| OBJECTIVE | RATE |
|---|---|
| **BASIC SKILLS** | |
| **READING** | |
| Personally assess reading comprehension skills and develop a personal strategy for continued improvement. | |
| Develop and reinforce critical reading skills. | |
| Respond to written directions clearly, legibly, and correctly. | |
| Receive, attend to, interpret, and respond to written messages and other cues. | |
| Locate, understand, and interpret written information from a variety of documents. | |
| Other | |
| **WRITING** | |
| Personally assess written communication skills and develop a personal strategy for continued improvement. | |
| Demonstrate the ability to utilize standard English, appropriate format, and logical order in practical writing. | |
| Create documents including graphs and flow charts to illustrate point. | |
| In writing, communicate ideas to justify positions; persuade and convince others. | |
| Create correspondence required in job seeking activities including letters and resumes. | |
| Utilizing technical knowledge, create documents of procedures or instructions. | |
| Other | |

Insert Form in Part V, Transferable Skills, Skills Investment Portfolio.

## Form 1-9 (Continued)

Rate the following skills between 1 and 5 in accordance to the importance for our graduates.

1 = no importance and 5 = extremely important

| ORAL COMMUNICATION | |
|---|---|
| Personally assess oral communication skills and develop a personal strategy for continued improvement. | |
| Formulate, communicate, and defend one's own beliefs. | |
| Receive, attend to, interpret, and respond to verbal messages and other cues. | |
| Summarize materials presented orally. | |
| Participate cooperatively as a team member, teaching, learning from, and negotiating with diverse members making a contribution to term success. | |
| Demonstrate ability to assess one's own skills and knowledge by responding to interview questions with specific personal examples. | |
| Ask clear questions to obtain desired information. | |
| Formally present technical information and respond to questions. | |
| Give a speech to persuade others of conclusions on complex topic. | |
| Other | |
| THINKING SKILLS | |
| Comprehend and use efficient learning techniques to acquire and apply knowledge. | |
| Specify goals and constraints, generate alternatives, consider risks, and evaluate and choose the best alternative. | |
| Recognize problems and devise and implement a plan of action. | |
| Discover a rule or principle underlying the relationship between two or more facts, events, or concepts and apply it to formulate a new conclusion. | |
| Compare and contrast two theories and select and defend one of the two. | |
| Develop and reinforce critical thinking processes. | |
| Develop and reinforce creative thinking processes. | |
| Utilizing the social science problem solving method, recognize problems and devise and implement a plan of action. | |
| Other | |
| | |
| | |

Insert Form in Part V, Transferable Skills, Skills Investment Portfolio.

## Form 1-9 (Continued)

Rate the following skills between 1 and 5 in accordance to the importance for our graduates.

1 = no importance and 5 = extremely important

| PERSONAL QUALITIES | |
|---|---|
| **RESPONSIBILITIES** | |
| Personally assess responsibilities and commitments and develop a personal strategy for continued improvement in fulfilling them. | |
| Exert a high level of effort and persevere toward goal attainment. | |
| Other | |
| **SELF ESTEEM** | |
| Believes in own self-worth and maintains a positive view of self. | |
| Maintain positive attitude. | |
| Demonstrate pride in self and projects. | |
| Other | |
| **SELF MANAGEMENT** | |
| Personally assess skills, knowledge, and motivation and develop a personal strategy for continued improvement. | |
| Allocate time and energy in completing projects in a timely manner. | |
| Take personal responsibility for obtaining skills, knowledge, and information required to accomplish task. | |
| Set personal goals and monitor progress. | |
| Exhibit self-control. | |
| Other | |
| **INTEGRITY AND HONESTY** | |
| Personally assess one's own values, beliefs and attitude and makes choices and acts in consistent manner. | |
| Represents facts honestly, fairly, and accurately. | |
| Respects property of others. | |
| Other | |

Insert Form in Part V, Transferable Skills, Skills Investment Portfolio.

# Form 1-9 (Continued)

Rate the following skills between 1 and 5 in accordance to the importance for our graduates.

1 = no importance and 5 = extremely important

| INFORMATION | |
|---|---|
| Demonstrate the ability to utilize a community or university library. | |
| Retrieve and organize data from a variety of sources, including computerized data bases, reference books, books, and periodicals. | |
| Identify need for data and select, retrieve, and analyze information and communicate the results to others in written, graphic, and pictorial format. | |
| Acquire and evaluate relevant information, and organize, maintain, analyze, interpret, communicate, and use applicable information. | |
| Present necessary information in logical sequence. | |
| Other | |
| **RESOURCES** | |
| Personally assess one's personal resources and allocates according to needs, commitment, and values. | |
| Monitors and allocates one's own time. | |
| Identifies requirement for resources to complete a project and allocate resources. | |
| Allocate duties of a small work team and institute a system to monitor for quality. | |
| Identifies requirement for resources to complete a project and obtains necessary resources. | |
| Other | |
| **INTERPERSONAL** | |
| Personally assess interpersonal skills and develop a personal strategy for continued improvement. | |
| Participate cooperatively as a team member, teaching, learning from, and negotiating with diverse members making a contribution to team success. | |
| Negotiate with others to accomplish a mutually beneficial solution. | |
| Demonstrate a respect for others and accepts cultural differences. | |
| Willing to teach others skills. | |
| Leads a small work team to accomplish an assigned task or project. | |

Insert Form in Part V, Transferable Skills, Skills Investment Portfolio.

## Form 1-9 (Continued)

Rate the following skills between 1 and 5 in accordance to the importance for our graduates.

1 = no importance and 5 = extremely important

| INTERPERSONAL (CONTINUED) | |
|---|---|
| Maintains an open mind in discussing controversial topics. | |
| Demonstrate skill to resolve differences that occur on small work teams. | |
| Other | |
| **OTHER NECESSARY SKILLS FOR SUCCESS** | |
| Other | |
| Other | |

Add skills rated 5 to your Disc Resume for Windows.

Insert Form in Part V, Transferable Skills, Skills Investment Portfolio.

71

Insert Form in Part V, Transferable Skills, Skills Investment Portfolio.

72

**Form 1-10**
**Proof By Example**

Name:_____          Date:_____

| SKILL (I Can) | PROOF (Example That Proves) |
|---|---|
|  |  |
|  |  |
|  |  |
|  |  |
|  |  |
|  |  |
|  |  |
|  |  |
|  |  |
|  |  |

Insert Form in Part V, Self Assessment, S.K.I.P.

Insert Form in Part V, Self Assessment, S.K.I.P.

**Form 1-11**
**Personal Information Reference Sheet**

Name: _____ Date: _____

Full Name: _____

Mailing Address: _____

_____

City            State      ZIP Code

Phone Number: _____

Employment Desired:
Position: _____

Available Hours: _____

Starting Date: _____

Salary Requirements: _____    _____    _____
                (Weekly)        (Hourly)       (Annually)

| Elementary School Name and Address | Attended From Month   Year | To Month   Year | Degree | Honors |
|---|---|---|---|---|
|  |  |  |  |  |
| High School Name and Address | Attended From Month   Year | To Month   Year | Degree | Honors |
|  |  |  |  |  |
| College Name and Address | Attended From Month   Year | To Month   Year | Degree | Honors |
|  |  |  |  |  |
| Additional Training Type and Address | Attended From Month   Year | To Month   Year | Degree | Honors |
|  |  |  |  |  |

Insert Form in Part VII, Job Application, S.K.I.P.

## Form 1-11 (Continued)
## Personal Information Reference Sheet

Military service:_____    Rank:_____

Dates:_____

| | FORMER EMPLOYERS | | | | |
|---|---|---|---|---|---|
| Dates From/ To | Employer Name and Address | Position | Duties | Beginning and Ending Salary | Reason for Leaving |
| | | | | | |
| | | | | | |
| | | | | | |
| | | | | | |
| | | | | | |

References    (1)    _____
                     Name/Address                           Phone
             (2)    _____
                     Name/Address                           Phone
             (3)    _____
                     Name/Address                           Phone

In case of emergency, contact:_____

Insert Form in Part VII, Job Application, S.K.I.P.

**Form 1-12**
**Goal Analysis**

Name:_____        Date:_____

Lifestyle -- Goals that support your living preferences.

- Where do you prefer to live (city, suburbs, country) and in what kind of space (apartment, condominium, townhouse, single- or multi-family house, mobile home)?

- With whom do you want to live (extended/immediate family, roommates, friends, no one)?

- Do you prefer conveniences such as off-street parking, laundry, dishwasher, or health club?

- Do you prefer cable TV, books, a stereo?

- What do you like to do in your leisure time?

- What kind of car would you like to drive?

Now arrange your goals according to the five categories listed above (personal, family, school/career, financial lifestyle). In the space provided, think of five goals set for yourself in each category. Later on you'll have the chance to select one goal from each category and establish concrete steps towards achieving them.

| PERSONAL GOALS | |
|---|---|
| **Current** | Future |
| 1. | |
| 2. | |
| 3. | |
| 4. | |
| 5. | |

Insert Form in Part VI, Employment Decision-Making, S.K.I.P.

77

**Form 1-12 (Continued)**

| FAMILY GOALS | |
|---|---|
| Current | Future |
| 1. | |
| 2. | |
| 3. | |
| 4. | |
| 5. | |

| SCHOOL/CAREER GOALS | |
|---|---|
| Current | Future |
| 1. | |
| 2. | |
| 3. | |
| 4. | |
| 5. | |

| FINANCIAL GOALS | |
|---|---|
| Current | Future |
| 1. | |
| 2. | |
| 3. | |
| 4. | |
| 5. | |

Insert Form in Part VI, Employment Decision-Making, S.K.I.P.

**Form 1-12 (Continued)**

| LIFESTYLE GOALS | |
|---|---|
| **Current** | Future |
| 1. | |
| 2. | |
| 3. | |
| 4. | |
| 5. | |

Insert Form in Part VI, Employment Decision-Making, S.K.I.P.

79

Insert Form in Part VI, Employment Decision-Making, S.K.I.P.

80

## Form 1-13
## Review Mission Statement and Revise if Necessary

Name: _____ Date: _____

_____

_____

_____

_____

_____

_____

_____

_____

_____

_____

_____

_____

_____

_____

Insert Form in Part VI, Employment Decision-Making, S.K.I.P.

Insert Form in Part VI, Employment Decision-Making, S.K.I.P.

82

## Form 1-14

Name:_____     Date:_____

Review and revise your career objective (See Form 1-2) after analyzing the new information you've generated.

## CAREER OBJECTIVE

_____

_____

_____

_____

_____

_____

_____

_____

Add to your Disc Resume for Windows.

Insert Form in Part VII, Resumes, S.K.I.P.

## Form 1-15
## Detailed Skill Analysis

Name:_____ Date:_____

Example:

| Ohm's Law | 1st Qtr. | Success Orientation | Draw Think Link diagram |
|-----------|----------|---------------------|-------------------------|

| What Do You Know (Principles and Concepts) | Date | Where | Proof By Example |
|--------------------------------------------|------|-------|------------------|
|  |  |  |  |
|  |  |  |  |
|  |  |  |  |
|  |  |  |  |
|  |  |  |  |

Insert Form in Part V, Self Assessment, S.K.I.P.

**Form 1-15**
**Detailed Skill Analysis (Continued)**

Name:_____ Date:_____

Example:

| Write Clear Definition | 3rd Qtr. | Written Commu- nications | Write example |
|---|---|---|---|

| What Do You Know (Principles and Concepts) | Date | Where | Proof By Example |
|---|---|---|---|
| | | | |
| | | | |
| | | | |
| | | | |
| | | | |
| | | | |

## Assignment for Portfolio 1-7

Examine the resumes on the following pages and review the advantages, disadvantages, and examples of various types of resumes in **WRITTEN COMMUNICATIONS RESOURCE DIGEST** (pages 356-368 in the Second edition) to determine which style of resume works best for you. Prepare a full resume, utilizing the style of your choice and the information you have just updated. Please review the following models and guidelines before proceeding.

After you have completed your resume, remember to do the following:
1. Use Spellcheck feature on your computer;
2. Use Grammarcheck feature on your computer; and
3. Check all company names for accuracy.

Proper spelling, grammar and format are critical in representing yourself professionally to a potential employer.

# Model 1-1
## CHRONOLOGICAL RESUME

---

### KRISTIN ALLISON JONES
11567 East 17th Street
Spokane, WA 01435
(509) 456-4587

**OBJECTIVE**

Looking to obtain a fulfilling and career oriented position in Computer Aided Drafting.

**EDUCATION**

**ITT Technical Institute**

San Antonio, TX

*Associate of Applied Science Degree*

September 1998

Computer Aided Drafting Technology.

Drafting courses in Architectural, Civil, Structural, and Piping.

**Honors graduate: 3.6 GPA.**

**University of Mary-Hardin Baylor**

Belton, TX

*Business Management*

Aug. 93 to May 95

2 years on Varsity Fastpitch Softball team

**EXPERIENCE**

**TAD Temporary Services**

San Antonio, TX

*Data Base Manager*

Sept. 97 to Present

Manage a Pharmaceutical Database

Responsible for the input of data files from U.S. Military Sites. Also, the editing for the database and query reports. Correspondence between analyst and programmer.

**Redner's Warehouse Market**

Reading, PA

*Assistant Manager*

Apr. 96 to Dec. 96

Responsible for opening and closing of the store. Performed customer service duties, inventory, and the upkeep of the merchandise on the floor.

**Evan Picone**

Reading, PA

*Stock Clerk*

Oct. 95 to Apr. 96

Was part of a team that performed manual labor to unload trucks, place freight in aisles, and stock shelves appropriately. I was also the emergency cashier.

**ManTech International**

San Antonio, TX

*Computer Tape Librarian*

June 95 to Oct. 95

Performed librarian duties in the Computer MegaCenter on Kelly Air Force Base.

**REFERENCES**

Available upon request.

---

Insert Model in Part VII, Resumes, S.K.I.P.

## TIMOTHY MILLER
123 Foxridge Drive
Crete Park, IL 60417
(777) 728-6969

**OBJECTIVE**

To achieve personal success in business through learning, combining my skills & experience using Desktop Publishing & Computer Aided Drafting technology.

**COMPUTER SKILLS**

Macintosh, Hewlett Packard & IBM Computer systems

Hammer Hard Drive systems, Syquest & Zip drive systems, color printers, laser enhanced scanner systems, Xerox copiers, plain paper & thermal type fax machines.

**SOFTWARE**

Microsoft Word, Excel, Access, Exchange, Windows NT & Win 95, MS-DOS, Pagemaker, Powerpoint, Norton Utilities, Adobe Photoshop, Illustrator, Corel Draw, Visionlab, Macromind Director, Typestyler, Autocad R13 & R14.

**EMPLOYMENT**

**Southwestern Bell/Adecco Employment Agency,** San Antonio, Texas

*Long Distance Database Administrator,* 02/98 - 05/98

Client Information Database Administration

In charge of data input for all sales in relation to long distance usage by clients using payphones within a five state format. Created Carrier Reports for USLD and AT & T. Required to update their customer base information network.

Software used: Microsoft Access, Microsoft Exchange, Word & Excel.

**Jana Inc., Assignment/Adecco Employment Agency**, San Antonio, Texas

*CAD Operator,* 08/97 - 02/98

Fedex Project (A300, A600-610) Airbuses

Draw schematic diagrams of technical modifications for repair manuals in accordance with contract specifications using a digitizer board, software and a mouse.

Software used: Autocad R13 & R14, Autovision

**Triborough Bridge and Tunnel Authority**, Randall's Island, New York

*Principal Administrative Assistant,* 12/90 - 05/96

Internal Security Department (Technical support, audio/visual, Special Investigations Divisions)

Assisted the Chief of ISD with priority administrative functions.

Provided support to managerial personnel in researching, developing, organizing and analyzing data for reports, charts, surveys and procedures.

Designed and maintained databases for special toll tickets, equipment purchases, Authority wide identification cards, master keys and contractor files.

Managed and safeguarded the administration of high security keys for the Authority and special toll tickets for department personnel.

Assisted in budgetary related responsibilities.

Prepared timecards and overtime reports for thirty-four (34) technicians.

Provided monthly status reports on all department expenditures.

**EDUCATION**

**ITT Technical Institute**, San Antonio, Texas

Computer Aid Drafting Technology - *Associate of Applied Science Degree*, September 1998

All drafting formats are taught and applied, including structural, civil, mechanical, piping, architectural, electrical, etc. Then the theories behind tolerances and design are reviewed through homework assignments and tests.

**REFERENCES**

Available upon request.

Insert Model in Part VII, Resumes, S.K.I.P.

## JOHN E. JONES

11567 East 17th Street

Spokane, WA 01435

(509) 456-4587

(Please leave message)

### OBJECTIVE

A position in Data Processing, preferably in Computer Operations or Programming. Five-Year Career Goal: Systems Analysis Management.

### SUMMARY OF QUALIFICATIONS

**COMPUTER SCIENCE, OPERATIONS & PROGRAMMING** -- Two years Computer Programming with emphasis in the following languages, software and operating systems: **BASIC, FORTRAN, COBOL, MS-DOS, LOTUS 1-2-3, DBASE III, SPF/PC, IBM OS/VS, JCL, AND CICS.**

**COMPUTER COMPUTATIONS/DATA PROCESSING** -- Eight years. Involved in all aspects of data retrieval from computations to design.

**MATHEMATICAL** -- Five years. Performed daily algebraic and trigonometric calculations.

**TEAMWORK** -- Eight years. Effectively and cooperatively worked in a fast-paced, demanding environment with all members of a surveying crew, as well as interacting with various executive key personnel.

**ADDITIONAL QUALIFICATIONS** -- Demonstrated ability to "debug" programs written by others. Developed training and instructional materials for software packages. Designed, set up, and operated PC-based data base for recordkeeping.

### EDUCATION

**SPOKANE TECHNICAL INSTITUTE,** Spokane, Washington 1988

672-hour course in Computer Programming and Operations. State certified. Graduated with honors. GPA: 3.67.

**WASHINGTON STATE UNIVERSITY,** Seattle, Washington 1987

Completed 15 semester hours in Computer Science which included the language of Fortran.

**SPOKANE SCHOOL OF SURVEYING & MAPPING,** Spokane, Washington, 1979

Certificate for 1,600-hour program.

### EMPLOYMENT BACKGROUND

Party Chief for the following companies:

Avery Structures, Inc., Spokane, Washington, 1990-93

Centennial Engineering, Seattle, Washington, 1988-90

J.R. Developers, Tacoma, Washington, 1986-88

Al Messahaq/ARAMCO, Saudi Arabia, 1982-86

Source: Robbins, Carolyn R., **THE JOB SEARCHER'S HANDBOOK**, Prentice Hall, 1997, 0-13-199621-5.

Insert Model in Part VII, Resumes, S.K.I.P.

**Guideline 1-12**
**Your Chronological Resume**

**NAME**
Address
Phone
E-Mail

_____(Career Objective)_____

_____

_____(Summary Experience)_____

Most recent:___Dates_____Place_____Duties_____

_____

_____

_____

_____(Education)_____

Most recent:___Dates_____College Degree_____

_____

_____

**References provided on request.**

**Guideline 1-13**
Your Functional Resume

**NAME**
Address
Phone
E-Mail

**Career Objective**

_____ **(Education)**_____

**Most recent:__First date_____College_____Degree_____**

_____

_____

_____**(Professional Experience)**_____

_____**(Usually divided by topics)**_____

_____

_____

_____

_____**(Employment History)**_____

**Most recent:___Date_____Place_____**

_____

_____

**References provided on request.**

_____

**Guideline 1-14**
**Your Combination Resume**

## NAME
Address
Phone
E-Mail

Objective

_____(Summary Qualifications)_____

_____

_____

_____

_____(Education)_____

Most recent:___Dates_____College Degree_____

_____

_____

_____

_____(Employment)_____

Most recent:___Dates_____Place_____Functions_____

_____

_____

**References provided on request.**

## Form 1-16
## Critique Your Resume

Name:_____ Date: _____

Use the following resume checklist and critique form to evaluate your resume.

|  | Strong | Average | Weak | Plans For Improvement |
|---|---|---|---|---|
| ✔ *Resume format.* Does it say "READ ME"? |  |  |  |  |
| ✔ *Appearance.* Is it brief? Did you use an interesting layout? Type clearly? Use a correct format? |  |  |  |  |
| ✔ *Length.* Are the key points concise? |  |  |  |  |
| ✔ *Significance.* Did you select your most relevant experiences? |  |  |  |  |
| ✔ *Communication.* Do your words give the "visual impression you want? Is the job objective clearly stated? |  |  |  |  |
| ✔ *Conciseness.* Does your information focus on the experiences that qualify you for the position? |  |  |  |  |
| ✔ *Completeness.* Did you include all important information? Have you made a connection between the job desired and your experience? |  |  |  |  |
| ✔ *Reality.* Does the resume represent you well enough to get you an interview? |  |  |  |  |
| ✔ *Skills.* Does your resume reflect the skills necessary for the job? |  |  |  |  |
| ✔ *Target employer.* Does your resume address the employer's situation? |  |  |  |  |

Source: Sukiennik - Bendat - Raufman, **THE CAREER PROGRAM: EXERCISING YOUR OPTIONS**, 5/e, Prentice Hall, 1998, 0-13-780826-7

Insert Form in Part VII, Resumes, S.K.I.P.

Insert Form in Part VII, Resumes, S.K.I.P.

## Assignment for Portfolio 1-8

Name:_____     Date:_____

Your instructor may ask you to prepare additional resumes using alternative formats. Once you've completed preparing such a resume, ask yourself the following:

Identify the format: _____

What are the advantages of this format?

_____

_____

_____

_____

_____

_____

_____

What are the disadvantages of this format?

_____

_____

_____

_____

_____

_____

Your answer should take into account your current qualification and experience.

Insert Assignment in Part VII, Resumes, S.K.I.P.

**Form 1-17**
**Skill Development Intention**

Name:_____     Date:_____

Now, go back and review the skills that you need to develop in order to improve the quality and effectiveness of your resume.

| SKILL DEVELOPMENT INTENTION | |
|---|---|
| **SKILL TO BE DEVELOPED** | **ACTION PLAN** |
| | |
| | |
| | |
| | |
| | |
| | |
| | |
| | |

Insert Form in Part V, Self Assessment, S.K.I.P.

# PART II

# ECONOMICS

## Guideline 2-1
## Problem-Solving Method

Remember that almost any situation you face, lends itself to problem-solving analysis/trouble-shooting. Economics is a discipline that provides another tool in your problem-solving arsenal.

Let's take a moment to review the problem-solving/trouble-shooting method. For more information, you may wish to review Chapter 3 in **PATHWAY TO SUCCESS,** Volume I.

There are several varieties of the problem-solving method. Please use the following for this exercise.

I.      DEVELOP PROBLEM-SOLVING STATEMENT. This statement clearly identifies the problem that is to be solved.

II.     ANALYZE THE PROBLEM.
                Investigate the cost and/or degree of problem (opportunity cost)
                        Use observation
                        Research the literature
                        Examine others' opinion or perception (Survey, Poll)
                Examine possible causes
                Correlate with other related problems
                Clarify dimensions of the problem
                Analyze the resistance to solving the problem

III.    DEVELOP POSSIBLE SOLUTIONS. Examine possible solutions or ways to decrease the problem. Include how the solution would be implemented.

IV.     SET A CRITERION FOR THE BEST SOLUTION. Set a list of characteristics that will be included in any solution.

V.      EXPLORE EACH SOLUTION. Apply criterion to the possible solutions. Evaluate each possible solution as it relates to the criteria.

VI.     SELECT THE BEST SOLUTION OR COMBINATION OF SOLUTIONS. Examine which solution most closely matches the criterion. You may be able to combine solutions to obtain more desired results. (NOTE: If criterion does not aid in the selection of best solution, the criterion or the solutions may be too general.)

What follows is a set of forms that you can use as you deal with problem-solving situations. If you need to make additional copies, please do so.

Insert Guideline in Part III, Problem Solving Method, S.K.I.P.

Insert Guideline in Part III, Problem Solving Method, S.K.I.P.

## Form 2-1

Name:_____   Date:_____

| PROBLEM SOLVING EXERCISE | |
|---|---|
| STEP | YOUR RESPONSE |
| **1. State the problem clearly.**<br>(State a problem you haven't resolved.) | |
| **2. Analyze the problem.**<br>(How does this problem impact you?) | |
| **3. Brainstorm possible solutions.**<br>(Explore as many options as you can.) | |
| **4. Determine the criteria for your solution.**<br>(Name the measures you will use for determining the effectiveness of your solutions.) | |
| **5. Explore each solution.**<br>(Discuss the negative and positive effects of your ideas. Match them to the criteria.) | |
| **6. Choose and execute the solution you decide is best.**<br>(How will you apply the solution?) | |

Insert Form in Part III, Problem Solving Method, S.K.I.P.

## Form 2-1

Name:_____    Date:_____

| PROBLEM SOLVING EXERCISE | |
|---|---|
| STEP | YOUR RESPONSE |
| **1. State the problem clearly.** (State a problem you haven't resolved.) | |
| **2. Analyze the problem.** (How does this problem impact you?) | |
| **3. Brainstorm possible solutions.** (Explore as many options as you can.) | |
| **4. Determine the criteria for your solution.** (Name the measures you will use for determining the effectiveness of your solutions.) | |
| **5. Explore each solution.** (Discuss the negative and positive effects of your ideas. Match them to the criteria.) | |
| **6. Choose and execute the solution you decide is best.** (How will you apply the solution?) | |

Insert Form in Part III, Problem Solving Method, S.K.I.P.

## Form 2-1

Name:_____ Date:_____

| PROBLEM SOLVING EXERCISE | |
|---|---|
| STEP | YOUR RESPONSE |
| **1. State the problem clearly.**<br>(State a problem you haven't resolved.) | |
| **2. Analyze the problem.**<br>(How docs this problem impact you?) | |
| **3. Brainstorm possible solutions.**<br>(Explore as many options as you can.) | |
| **4. Determine the criteria for your solution.**<br>(Name the measures you will use for determining the effectiveness of your solutions.) | |
| **5. Explore each solution.**<br>(Discuss the negative and positive effects of your ideas. Match them to the criteria.) | |
| **6. Choose and execute the solution you decide is best.**<br>(How will you apply the solution?) | |

Insert Form in Part III, Problem Solving Method, S.K.I.P.

## Form 2-1

Name:_____ Date:_____

| PROBLEM SOLVING EXERCISE | |
|---|---|
| STEP | YOUR RESPONSE |
| **1. State the problem clearly.**<br>(State a problem you haven't resolved.) | |
| **2. Analyze the problem.**<br>(How does this problem impact you?) | |
| **3. Brainstorm possible solutions.**<br>(Explore as many options as you can.) | |
| **4. Determine the criteria for your solution.**<br>(Name the measures you will use for determining the effectiveness of your solutions.) | |
| **5. Explore each solution.**<br>(Discuss the negative and positive effects of your ideas. Match them to the criteria.) | |
| **6. Choose and execute the solution you decide is best.**<br>(How will you apply the solution?) | |

Insert Form in Part III, Problem Solving Method, S.K.I.P.

## Introduction

Jobs are like other commodities, they are subject to the laws of supply and demand.

You need to assess your goals and objectives, the situation in your local community, and the opportunities that exist elsewhere in order to make good economic choices.

The first step in making good economic choices is gathering data. For example in the area of job choice:

✔      Personal goals and objectives

✔      Budget information

✔      Values

✔      Job requirements

✔      Job opportunities

✔      Other preferences

Insert Introduction in Part VI, Employment Decision-Making, S.K.I.P.

Insert Introduction in Part VI, Employment Decision-Making, S.K.I.P.

## Guideline 2-2
## Budgeting

### How Can You Create A Budget That Works?

Every time you have some money in your pocket and have to figure out whether it will pay for what you want at that moment, you are budgeting your money. Consider your resources (money coming in) and expenditures (money flowing out). A smart budget adjusts the money flow for the best possible chance that what comes in will be more than what goes out. Smart budgeting is a worthwhile investment in your future.

### The Art of Budgeting

Budgeting involves following a few basic steps in order. These steps are:

- Determine how much money you make
- Determining how much money you spend
- Subtracting the second number (what you spend) from the first number (what you make)
- Evaluating the result
- Making decisions about how to adjust your spending or earning based on that result

Budgeting regularly is easiest. Use a specified time frame, such as a week or month. Most people budget on a month-by-month basis.

### Determine How Much You Will Make

Do this by adding up all your money receipts -- job income, financial aid and so on. Be sure, when you are figuring your income, to use the amounts that remain *after* taxes have been taken out.

### Figure Out How Much You Spend

You may or may not have a handle on your spending. Many people don't take the time to keep track. If you have never before paid much attention to how you spend money, examine your spending patterns (you will have an opportunity to do this in the applications for this chapter). Over a month's time, record expenditures in a small notebook or on a piece of paper on a home bulletin board. You don't have to list everything down to the penny. Just indicate expenditures over five dollars, making sure to count smaller expenditures if they are frequent (a bus pass for a month, soda or newspaper purchases per week). In your list, include an estimate of the following:

- Rent/mortgage/school room fees
- Tuition or educational loan payments (divide your annual total by 12 to arrive at a monthly figure)

(Continued)

## Guideline 2-2 (Continued)
## Budgeting

- Books, lab fees, and other educational expenses
- Regular bills (heat, gas, electric, phone, car payment, water)
- Credit card or other payments on credit
- Food, clothing, toiletries, and household supplies
- Child care
- Entertainment and related items (eating out, books and publications, movies)
- Health, auto, and home/renters' insurance
- Transportation and auto expenses

Subtract what you spend from what you make. Ideally, you will have a positive number. You may end up with a negative number, however, especially if you haven't made a habit of keeping track of your spending. This indicates that you are spending more than you make, which over a long period of time is a problem.

### Evaluate the Result
After you arrive at your number, determine what it tells you. If you have a positive number, decide how to save it if you can. If you end up with a negative number, ask yourself questions about what is causing the deficit -- where you are spending too much or earning too little. Of course, surprise expenses during some months may cause you to spend more than usual, such as if you have to replace your refrigerator, pay equipment fees for a particular course, or have an emergency medical procedure. However, when a negative number comes up for what seems to be a typical month, you may need to adjust your budget over the long term.

### Make Decisions About How to Adjust Spending or Earning
Looking at what may cause you to overspend, brainstorm possible solutions that address those causes. Solutions can involve either increasing resources or decreasing spending. To deal with spending, prioritize your expenditures and trim the ones you really don't need to make. Do you eat out too much? Can you live without cable, a beeper, a cellular phone? Be smart. Cut out unaffordable extras. As for resources, investigate ways to take in more money. Taking a part-time job, hunting down scholarships or grants, or increasing hours at a current job may help.

### A Sample Budget
The following table shows a sample budget of an unmarried student living with two other students. It will give you an idea of how to budget (all expenditures are general estimates, based on averages).

To make up the $190 that this student went over budget, he can adjust his spending. He could rent movies or check them out of the library instead of going to the theater. He could socialize with friends at someone's apartment instead of paying high prices and tips at a bar or restaurant. Instead of buying CDS and tapes, he could borrow them. He could also shop for specials and bargains in the grocery store or go to a warehouse supermarket to stock up on staples at discount prices. He could make his lunch instead of buying it and walk instead of taking public transportation.

Insert Guideline in Part III, Resources, S.K.I.P.

## Guideline 2-2 (Continued)
## Budgeting

## A Student's Sample Budget

| MONTHLY EXPENDITURES | AMOUNT |
|---|---|
| Tuition ($9,648 per year) | $ 804.00 |
| Public transportation | $ 90.00 |
| Phone | $ 40.00 |
| Food | $ 230.00 |
| Medical insurance | $ 120.00 |
| Rent (including utilities) | $ 300.00 |
| Entertainment/miscellaneous | $ 150.00 |
| **Total Expenses** | $1,734.00 |
| MONTHLY INCOME | AMOUNT |
| Salary (10.85 x 20 hours=217 x 4.33=940.33) | $ 940.33 |
| Student Loans | $ 804.00 |
| Total Income | $1,744.33 |
| **Balance** | $ 10.33 |

Not everyone likes the work involved in keeping a budget, but it is helpful. Even if you have to force yourself to do it, you will discover that budgeting can reduce stress and help you take control of your finances and your life. You can see that this student only has a $10 leadway.

## Savings Strategies

You can save money and still enjoy life. Make your fun less-expensive fun -- or save up for a while to splurge on a really special occasion. Here are some suggestions for saving a little bit of money here and there. Small amounts can add up to big savings after a while.

- Rent movies or attend bargain matinees.
- When safe for the fabric, hand-wash items you ordinarily dry-clean.
- Check movies, CDS, tapes, and books out of your library.

### Guideline 2-2 (Continued)
### Budgeting

- Make popcorn instead of buying bags of chips.
- Walk instead of paying for public transportation.
- If you have storage space, buy detergent, paper products, toiletries, and other staples in bulk.
- Shop in secondhand stores.
- Keep your possessions neat, clean, and properly maintained -- they will last longer.
- Take advantage of weekly supermarket specials and bring coupons when you shop.
- Reuse grocery bags for food storage and garbage instead of buying bags.
- Return bottles and cans for deposits if you live in a state that accepts them.
- Trade clothing with friends and barter services (plumbing for baby-sitting, for example).
- Buy display models of appliances or electronics (stereo equipment, TVS, VCRs).
- Take your lunch instead of buying it.
- Find a low-rate long distance calling plan, use e-mail, or write letters.
- Save on heat by dressing warmly and using blankets; save on air conditioning by using fans.
- Have pot-luck parties; ask people to bring dinner foods or munchies.

Add your own suggestions here!

_____

_____

_____

_____

_____

You can also maximize savings and minimize spending by using bank accounts and credit cards wisely.

**Form 2-2**
**Budgeting**

Name:_____     Date:_____

## MONTHLY PERSONAL BUDGET

**INCOME**

    Wages                    _____

    Tips                     _____

    *Loans                _____

    *Grants              _____

    *Scholarship       _____

    Other                 _____

                        _____

                        _____

*Divide total by amount covered

**TOTAL INCOME**                                  _____

**EXPENSES**

    Housing

        Rent                 _____

        House payments   _____

        Maintenance     _____

        Utilities         _____

    Tuition              _____

    Transportation

        Auto loan        _____

        Maintenance     _____

        Insurance        _____

        Public transportation  _____

        Gas estimate    _____

    Child care          _____

    Food

        Groceries        _____

        Restaurant/fast food  _____

    Medical insurance/expenses  _____

    Telephone          _____

    Clothing           _____

    Loan payments      _____

    Entertainment      _____

    Miscellaneous      _____

                        _____

**TOTAL EXPENSES**                           _____

                    + ( - )   _____

Insert Form in Part III, Resources, S.K.I.P.

ECONOMICS

Name: _____     Date: _____

**Form 2-3**
**Budgeting – Tracking Expenditures**

| EXPENSES | MONTH 1 | MONTH 2 | MONTH 3 |
|---|---|---|---|
| Housing: Rent | | | |
| House payments | | | |
| Maintenance | | | |
| Utilities | | | |
| Tuition | | | |
| Transportation: Auto loan | | | |
| Maintenance | | | |
| Insurance | | | |
| Public transportation | | | |
| Gas estimates | | | |
| Child care | | | |
| Food: Groceries | | | |
| Restaurant/Fast food | | | |
| Medical insurance/expenses | | | |
| Telephone | | | |
| Clothing | | | |
| Loan payments | | | |
| Entertainment | | | |
| Miscellaneous: | | | |
| | | | |
| **TOTAL EXPENSES** | | | |

Insert Form in Part III, Resources, S.K.I.P.

119

**Form 2-4**
**Quality of Life Inventory**

Name:_____     Date:_____

Interesting work, earnings, work environment, and location are important considerations to people making decisions about occupations and workplaces. Rate the following according to their importance to you -- 1 is low, 5 is high.

| | QUALITY OF LIFE INVENTORY | 1 | 2 | 3 | 4 | 5 |
|---|---|---|---|---|---|---|
| 1. | *Cost of living.* I prefer to live in an area where: | | | | | |
| | -State and local income and sales taxes are low (or nonexistent). | | | | | |
| | -Property taxes are reasonable. | | | | | |
| | -The cost of a house is low. | | | | | |
| | -Food costs are low or below average. | | | | | |
| | -Housing repairs, furniture, and appliances are low-priced. | | | | | |
| | -People can afford single-family homes. | | | | | |
| | -Utilities (gas, oil, electricity, water) are inexpensive. | | | | | |
| | -Mortgages and rents are reasonable. | | | | | |
| | -College expenses are low or moderate. | | | | | |
| | -Health care costs are low or below average. | | | | | |
| | **SUB-TOTAL** | | | | | |
| 2. | *Jobs.* I prefer to live in an area where: | | | | | |
| | -The population is growing rapidly or above the national average. | | | | | |
| | -The employment rate is high (or the unemployment rate is low). | | | | | |
| | -Employment growth is forecast to be high or above average. | | | | | |
| | -The business climate is good (lower taxes, welfare costs, and so on). | | | | | |

Insert Form in Part VI, Values, S.K.I.P.

## Form 2-4 (Continued)
Rate the following according to their importance to you -- 1 is low, 5 is high.

| | | | | | | |
|---|---|---|---|---|---|---|
| | -The economic climate and job outlook for an entire region of the country are good. | | | | | |
| | -The income growth rate is expected to be high or above average. | | | | | |
| | -Unemployment benefits are adequate or above average. | | | | | |
| | -There are "recession-resistant" industries; job security is good. | | | | | |
| | -Salaries are higher than the national average. | | | | | |
| | -Employers emphasize the quality of work and life. | | | | | |
| | **SUB-TOTAL** | | | | | |
| 3. | *Crime rate.* I prefer to live in an area where: | | | | | |
| | -The population is not crowded together; the area is not densely populated. | | | | | |
| | -There are fewer males aged 14 to 25 in relation to the rest of the population than in most areas. | | | | | |
| | -More middle-class and well-to-do- people than poor or poverty-stricken people live. | | | | | |
| | -There are strong ethnic neighborhoods. | | | | | |
| | -There is a stable population whose characteristics stay basically the same. | | | | | |
| | -The rates of arson, alcoholism, drug abuse, divorce, and suicide are low. | | | | | |
| | -The weather is cold or mild, but rarely hot and humid. | | | | | |
| | -The police force is considered strong and effective. | | | | | |
| | -Community attitudes favor tougher laws and stiffer sentences for criminals. | | | | | |
| | -Citizens and neighborhoods keep an eye out for each other's safety and property and offer information, identification, and testimony to help stop crime. | | | | | |
| | **SUB-TOTAL** | | | | | |

Insert Form in Part VI, Values, S.K.I.P.

**Form 2-4 (Continued)**
Rate the following according to their importance to you -- 1 is low, 5 is high.

| | | | | | | |
|---|---|---|---|---|---|---|
| 4. | *Health care and environment.* I prefer to live in an area where: | | | | | |
| | -There is an adequate supply of doctors in relation to the population. | | | | | |
| | -There are sufficient hospital beds in relation to the local population. | | | | | |
| | -There are medical schools and teaching hospitals. | | | | | |
| | -Medical costs are reasonable or low. | | | | | |
| | -There are cardiac rehabilitation centers or acute stroke centers. | | | | | |
| | -There are comprehensive cancer treatment centers. | | | | | |
| | -Drinking water is clean, free of chemical and organic pollutants. | | | | | |
| | -Fluoride is in the drinking water. | | | | | |
| | -There is clean air to breathe, a low degree of air pollution and smog. | | | | | |
| | -There is little or no ragweed pollen (or other allergens) in the air. | | | | | |
| | **SUB-TOTAL** | | | | | |
| 5. | *Transportation.* I prefer to live in an area where: | | | | | |
| | -There are airports and regular airline service. | | | | | |
| | -There is passenger rail service. | | | | | |
| | -There are interstate highways. | | | | | |
| | -The roads, streets, and freeways are not congested. | | | | | |
| | -There is a good public transportation system. | | | | | |
| | -There is a good road system, well-planned and well-maintained. | | | | | |
| | -Trucks and rail lines are routed away from heavily traveled car routes. | | | | | |
| | -Traffic laws are strongly enforced against drunk and reckless drivers. | | | | | |

Insert Form in Part VI, Values, S.K.I.P.

Rate the following according to their importance to you -- 1 is low, 5 is high.

| | | | | | | |
|---|---|---|---|---|---|---|
| | -The costs of owning and driving a car (insurance rates, taxes) are low. | | | | | |
| | -The life of a car is longer than average. | | | | | |
| | **SUB-TOTAL** | | | | | |
| 6. | *Education.* I prefer to live in an area where: | | | | | |
| | -The student-teacher ratio in schools is low; class sizes are small. | | | | | |
| | -More than an average amount of money is spent per student in schools. | | | | | |
| | -Teachers are paid an above-average salary, even if it means higher taxes. | | | | | |
| | -Many options for training and education are available in local colleges. | | | | | |
| | -Teachers are held accountable through good supervision and competency testing. | | | | | |
| | -There is a selection of private schools. | | | | | |
| | -Student absentee rates are low. | | | | | |
| | -There are many adult, continuing, or lifelong learning education programs. | | | | | |
| | -Tuition rates are low or reasonable in local colleges or private schools. | | | | | |
| | -The quality of education is considered to be excellent or above average. | | | | | |
| | **SUB-TOTAL** | | | | | |
| 7. | *The Arts.* I prefer to live in an area where: | | | | | |
| | -Colleges and universities make cultural contributions. | | | | | |
| | -There are symphony orchestras. | | | | | |
| | -There are opera companies or dance companies. | | | | | |
| | -There are theaters or acting companies. | | | | | |
| | -There are public television stations. | | | | | |
| | -Fine art radio stations offer classical music. | | | | | |

Insert Form in Part VI, Values, S.K.I.P.

Rate the following according to their importance to you -- 1 is low, 5 is high.

|  |  |  |  |  |  |  |
|---|---|---|---|---|---|---|
|  | -Art and natural-history museums are available. |  |  |  |  |  |
|  | -There are public libraries with a wide selection of books and services. |  |  |  |  |  |
|  | -Many artists, actors, authors, dancers, and musicians live. |  |  |  |  |  |
|  | -Quality newspapers are available. |  |  |  |  |  |
|  | **SUB-TOTAL** |  |  |  |  |  |
| 8. | *Recreation.* I prefer to live in an area where: |  |  |  |  |  |
|  | -There are many public or private golf courses. |  |  |  |  |  |
|  | -There are many bowling alleys. |  |  |  |  |  |
|  | -Above average amounts of money are spent on public parks and recreational facilities. |  |  |  |  |  |
|  | -There are movie theaters, television stations, and dramatic performances. |  |  |  |  |  |
|  | -There are neighborhood bars, pool halls, nightclubs, or social gatherings. |  |  |  |  |  |
|  | -There is a zoo or an aquarium. |  |  |  |  |  |
|  | -There is an amusement park or a family theme park. |  |  |  |  |  |
|  | -There are many sports events to attend. |  |  |  |  |  |
|  | -There are horse or dog race tracks or automobile race tracks. |  |  |  |  |  |
|  | -There are skiing facilities, hiking trails, beaches, or sailing opportunities. |  |  |  |  |  |
|  | **SUB-TOTAL** |  |  |  |  |  |
| 9. | *Climate (and terrain).* I prefer to live in an area where: |  |  |  |  |  |
|  | -I can establish my own kind of recreation and leisure time activities. |  |  |  |  |  |
|  | -I can keep heating and/or cooling costs down. |  |  |  |  |  |
|  | -The temperatures are mild, not too hot or too cold. |  |  |  |  |  |
|  | -The humidity does not get too high and uncomfortable. |  |  |  |  |  |
|  | -There is a lot of sunshine (or there is a lot of snow). |  |  |  |  |  |

Insert Form in Part VI, Values, S.K.I.P.

**Form 2-4 (Continued)**

Rate the following according to their importance to you -- 1 is low, 5 is high.

| | | | | | | |
|---|---|---|---|---|---|---|
| | -The weather is the same year-round (or the weather is changeable and varied). | | | | | |
| | -There is little risk of severe thunderstorms, hail, tornadoes, or hurricanes. | | | | | |
| | -There is little risk of earthquakes or floods. | | | | | |
| | -There are mountains and hills (or the terrain is mostly flat). | | | | | |
| | -There is a lot of vegetation, forest growth, and adequate rainfall. | | | | | |
| | **SUB-TOTAL** | | | | | |
| 10. | *Miscellaneous.* I prefer to live in an area where: | | | | | |
| | -There are churches or synagogues of my religious affiliation. | | | | | |
| | -There is good fire protection and quick response to fire alarms. | | | | | |
| | -There is a chapter of my professional association or labor union. | | | | | |
| | -There is a branch of my service club, lodge, or social group. | | | | | |
| | -Government is effective, offers good service, and operates efficiently. | | | | | |
| | -People are civic-minded and take pride in their community. | | | | | |
| | -There are fine restaurants. | | | | | |
| | -There are resources to help people find employment. | | | | | |
| | -There are many trees and shady places. | | | | | |
| | -(Add one item important to you but not on this list) | | | | | |
| | **SUB-TOTAL** | | | | | |

Insert Form in Part VI, Values, S.K.I.P.

## Form 2-4 (Continued)
## Quality of Life Inventory

**SCORING THE QUALITY OF LIFE INVENTORY**
Go back through the inventory, total each sub-category, and list the totals below.

| Category | Subtotal Points | Rank |
|---|---|---|
| 1. Costs of living | _____ | _____ |
| 2. Jobs | _____ | _____ |
| 3. Crime rate | _____ | _____ |
| 4. Health care and environment | _____ | _____ |
| 5. Transportation | _____ | _____ |
| 6. Education | _____ | _____ |
| 7. The Arts | _____ | _____ |
| 8. Recreation | _____ | _____ |
| 9. Climate | _____ | _____ |
| 10. Miscellaneous | _____ | _____ |

Review the items you rated five. These items reflect the quality areas most important to you in your personal quality of life assessment. What are the implications for your job selection process?

**Form 2-5**
**Goal Clarification**

Name:_____     Date: _____

(You may wish to review a similar form that you completed for Part 3 - Overcoming Obstacles - in your Portfolio.)

**PERSONAL GOALS**

1._____
2._____
3._____
4._____
5._____

**FAMILY GOALS**

1._____
2._____
3._____
4._____
5._____

**SCHOOL GOALS**

1._____
2._____
3._____
4._____
5._____

**FINANCIAL GOALS**

1._____
2._____
3._____
4._____
5._____

**LIFESTYLE GOALS**

1._____
2._____
3._____
4._____
5._____

**CAREER GOALS**

1._____
2._____
3._____
4._____
5._____

Insert Form in Part VI, Values, S.K.I.P.

**Assignment for Portfolio 2-1**
**Allocation of Resources**

Name:_____ Date:_____

## INTRODUCTION

Time is a valuable resource and you frequently make usage decisions about it. These decisions have economic implications. Therefore, it is important to understand what activities absorb your time.

## OBJECTIVE

Using skills learned in Success Orientation and in this class, develop a time allocation chart.

### TIME ALLOCATION:

☐   Complete the personal time allocation chart for one week.

☐   Based on the time allocation chart, develop a trial schedule.

☐   After trying the trial schedule, write a review of how well the schedule worked.

☐   Summarize what steps you will take to make effective use of your time. You may want to review the time management material in Chapter 3 of **PATHWAY TO SUCCESS**, Volume I.

Insert Assignment in Part III, Resources, S.K.I.P.

**Guideline 2-3**
**Time Allocation**

Name:_____ Date:_____

There are many different techniques designed to assist an individual to manage their time wisely. Everyone has the same amount of this resource.

| seconds | minutes | hours | days | weeks | months | year |
|---------|---------|-------|------|-------|--------|------|
| seconds | 60 | 360 | 8,640 | 60,480 | 262,060 | 3,144,960 |
| minutes | | 60 | 1,440 | 10,080 | 43,680 | 524,160 |
| hours | | | 24 | 168 | 728 | 8,736 |
| days | | | | 7 | 30.33 | 364 |
| weeks | | | | | 4.333 | 52 |
| months | | | | | | 12 |

Successful individuals develop a system to manage their time to achieve their goals. All of the systems require the setting of goals, and priorities realistically scheduling task and adjustment.

**Form 2-6**

Name:_____ Date:_____

**FILL IN THE FOLLOWING CHART FOR A TYPICAL WEEK**

| TASK | PRIORITY (1-High, 5-Low) | FIXED HOURS CANNOT CHANGE | FLEXIBLE HOURS CHOICE OF WHEN |
|---|---|---|---|
| **PERSONAL MAINTENANCE** | | | |
| SLEEP | | | |
| GROOMING | | | |
| EXERCISE | | | |
| EATING | | | |
| OTHER | | | |
| **ACADEMIC** | | | |
| CLASS | | | |
| STUDY GROUP | | | |
| PERSONAL STUDY | | | |
| OTHER | | | |
| **WORK** | | | |
| SCHEDULED TIME | | | |
| OVERTIME | | | |
| SECOND JOB | | | |
| OVERTIME | | | |
| OTHER | | | |
| **HOME AND FAMILY** | | | |
| CHORES | | | |
| FAMILY SUPPORT | | | |
| SHOPPING | | | |
| OTHER | | | |

Insert Form in Part III, Resources, S.K.I.P.

**Form 2-6 (Continued)**

Name:_____ Date:_____

| TRAVEL | | | |
|---|---|---|---|
| TO/FROM COLLEGE | | | |
| TO/FROM JOB | | | |
| OTHER | | | |
| RECREATION | | | |
| ORGANIZED TEAMS | | | |
| OTHER | | | |
| SPIRITUAL/COMMUNITY SERVICE | | | |
| ORGANIZED | | | |
| COMMITMENT | | | |
| OTHER | | | |
| OTHER COMMITMENTS | | | |
| | | | |
| | | | |
| **TOTAL HOURS** | | | |

Insert Form in Part III, Resources, S.K.I.P.

**Assignment for Portfolio 2-2**
**Research**

Name:_____ Date:_____

**OBJECTIVE:**
 Compare and contrast economic factors of employment opportunities in your community and another community that is in another region of the country.

**METHOD:**

**STEP #1:**
|    |                                                        |
|----|--------------------------------------------------------|
| A. | Determine possible job opportunities.                  |
| B. | Determine cost of living.                              |
| C. | Determine how each city matches the quality of life assessment. |
| D. | Determine how each city matches your goals and preferences. |

**STEP #2:**
 List at least five companies in each region that are potential employers.

Insert Assignment in Part VI, Employment Decision-Making, S.K.I.P.

Insert Assignment in Part VI, Employment Decision-Making, S.K.I.P.

## Assignment for Portfolio 2-3
## Team Project

Name:_____ Date:_____

### OBJECTIVES:

Utilizing the economic method and tools, analyze and recommend a solution to a contemporary problem.

Participate as a member of a team and contribute to successful completion of a project.

Allocate duties of a small work team and institute a system to monitor for quality.

Acquire, organize, interpret, and evaluate information from a variety of sources.

Demonstrate the ability to communicate effectively and correctly in writing.

Cooperatively work on a team.

### METHOD:

Utilizing the problem solving method, your team will select, analyze a problem that has economic impact, set a standard or criteria for best solutions, analyze possible solutions, and develop a recommended solution.

Write a team report which demonstrates the ability to use the problem-solving method and economic way of thinking. Proofread for grammatical errors and logical style.

Be sure to:
1. Include economic concepts
2. Use appropriate economic methods and tools
3. Apply appropriate depth of analysis
4. Deliver correct written presentation

Insert Assignment in Part III, Problem Solving Method, S.K.I.P.

Insert Assignment in Part III, Problem Solving Method, S.K.I.P.

**Form 2-7**
**Peer Evaluation Team Project**

Name:_____ Date:_____

Your major contribution:

| TEAM MEMBER | CONTRIBUTION |
|---|---|
|  |  |

Rank each team member according to their contribution: 1 - being given to the most valuable team member.

**Form 2-8**
**Group Process**

GROUP _____

EVALUATOR _____

### PROJECT EVALUATION FORM

Each student will evaluate the group process twice during the quarter. The first evaluation must be turned in anytime during weeks 2-6. The second must be turned in anytime during weeks 7-11.

Circle the number that best reflects your evaluation of your group. Include comments beneath each question.

1.  There was regular and consistent participation by most members.
    Yes          1     2     3     4     5     6     7     No
    Comments:

2.  Members showed signs of listening (paraphrasing, responding to points made, summarizing other's points, nodding).
    Always     1     2     3     4     5     6     7     Never
    Comments:

3.  Members appeared to be prepared for the meeting.
    Prepared     1     2     3     4     5     6     7     Unprepared
    Comments:

4.  Discussion was focused and stayed on the topic or task.
    Always     1     2     3     4     5     6     7     Never
    Comments:

Insert Form in Part IV, Group Dynamics, S.K.I.P.

## PROJECT EVALUATION FORM (Continued)

5.    Members' statements were clear, brief, and easy to follow.
       Always       1      2      3      4      5      6      7      Never
       Comments:

6.    Group appears able to use the best techniques or procedure for managing meeting focus.
       Always       1      2      3      4      5      6      7      Never
       Comments:

7.    Members' evaluations and criticism were phrased constructively.
       Always       1      2      3      4      5      6      7      Never
       Comments:

8.    Members appeared to work in a cooperative manner.
       Always       1      2      3      4      5      6      7      Never
       Comments:

9.    Members were willing to offer opinions, ask questions, and contribute to discussion.
       Always       1      2      3      4      5      6      7      Never
       Comments:

10.    Evaluation of opinions, ideas, proposals, and information was thorough and carefully done.
       Always       1      2      3      4      5      6      7      Never
       Comments:

11.    Relationships among members appeared to be friendly and respectful.
       Always       1      2      3      4      5      6      7      Never
       Comments:

---

Insert Form in Part IV, Group Dynamics, S.K.I.P.

## PROJECT EVALUATION FORM (Continued)

12.    Members volunteered to perform group tasks.
       Always        1      2      3      4      5      6      7      Never
       Comments:


13.    Members followed through with assignments.
       Yes           1      2      3      4      5      6      7      No
       Comments:


14.    All members are contributing to the success of this group.
       Yes           1      2      3      4      5      6      7      No
       Comments:


15.    The overall group process is working.
       Yes           1      2      3      4      5      6      7      No
       Comments:

---

Insert Form in Part IV, Group Dynamics, S.K.I.P.

# PART III

# SOCIOLOGY

## Introduction

The decision to work is more than just an economic one; it has huge sociological implications. It's important for you to understand this and to utilize your understanding of sociology, yourself, your family, and your personal goals and objectives to make good decisions regarding your job choice and potential employers. Your job decision will effect every level of your life, so it is important not only to understand yourself, and your goals, but to also research companies and industries carefully and to apply problem-solving skills to all the information in your possession.

Change is another important issue. It is a constant in our society and you will deal with it throughout your life. Look at the following chart to see some of the ways it can affect you.

Insert Introduction in Part VI, Personal Objectives, S.K.I.P.

146

## Guideline 3-1
### PERSONAL CHANGE PRODUCES NEW PRIORITIES

| CHANGE | EFFECTS AND CHANGED NEEDS | NEW PRIORITIES |
| --- | --- | --- |
| Lost job | Loss of income; need for others in your household to contribute more income | Job hunting; reduction in your spending; additional training or education in order to qualify for a different job |
| New job | Change in daily/weekly schedule; need for increased contribution of household help from others | Time and energy commitment to new job, maintaining confidence, learning new skills |
| Started school | Fewer hours for work, family, and personal time; responsibility for classwork; need to plan semesters ahead of time | Careful scheduling; making sure you have time to attend class and study adequately; strategic planning of classes and of career goals |
| Relationship/marriage | Responsibility toward your partner; merging of your schedules and perhaps your finances and belongings | Time and energy commitment to relationship |
| Break-up/divorce | Change in responsibility for any children; increased responsibility for your own finances; possible a need to relocate; increased independence | Making time for yourself, gathering support from friends and family, securing your finances, making sure you have your own income |
| Bought car | Responsibility for monthly payment; responsibility for upkeep | Regular income so that you can make payments on time; time and money for upkeep |
| New baby | Increased parenting responsibility; need money to pay for baby's needs or if you had to stop working; need help with other children | Child care, flexible employment, increased commitment from a partner or other supporter |
| New cultural environment (from new home, job, or school) | Exposure to unfamiliar people and traditions; tendency to keep to yourself | Learning about the culture with which you are now interacting; openness to new relationships |

Insert Guideline in Part III, Problem Solving Method, S.K.I.P.

## Guideline 3-1A
## SOCIAL CHANGE PRODUCES NEW PRIORITIES

The chart below indicates social change and briefly lists some of the effects and the changes in priorities. There is space for additional social changes.

| SOCIAL CHANGE | PARTIAL LIST OF EFFECTS AND CHANGED NEEDS | PARTIAL LIST OF NEW PRIORITIES |
|---|---|---|
| Increase in working mothers Increase in single parent homes | Decline of family, increased need for child care. | Quality child care. Importance of quality family time. |
| Economic globalization | Loss of jobs to other markets, greater cultural diversity, ability to change jobs. | Increase in marketable and flexible skills; increase cultural understanding. |
| Information Revolution | Access to large amounts of information. Cultural lag between those with access and those without. | Skilled in information retrieval. Security and privacy issues. Access to computer and Internet. Parent responsibility with children on Internet. |
| Work or quality teams | Change in job responsibilities and required skills | Empowerment of worker to contribute to greater good. Development of critical thinking and communication skills. |
| Aging of America | More dependent adults | New alternatives for care of seniors |
| Increase in secularization | Change of influence of church | Values taught in other institutions |
| | | |
| | | |
| | | |

Insert Guideline in Part III, Problem Solving Method, S.K.I.P.

**Assignment for Portfolio 3-1**
**Outline for Summary**

## ARTICLE REVIEW

**OBJECTIVES (Scans):**

- Locate, retrieve, analyze, and interpret written information.

- Formulate an opinion based on facts and accepted concepts and communicate and defend opinion in writing.

I.    IDENTIFICATION OF ARTICLE

     A.    Subject

     B.    Article title

     C.    Author (if listed)

     D.    Magazine title

     E.    Date of magazine

     F.    Page number(s)

II.   SUMMARY OF ARTICLE

     A.    Author's main point(s) or purpose

     B.    Supporting examples or data

     C.    Author bias

III.  APPLICATION TO LIFE
(How does the article apply to life, goals, or specific challenges and/or career of choice.)

IV.   STUDENT OPINION

     A.    Agreement/disagreement with author's point or view (Do you agree or disagree with the author?)

     B.    Support of opinion
(Defend your opinion.)

     C.    Recommendation of article
(Would you recommend this article and why?)

Insert Assignment in Part IV, Written Skills, S.K.I.P.

**Assignment for Portfolio 3-1 (Continued)**
**Summary Criteria Checklist**

✔   Does your summary provide the works cited information for the article that you're summarizing?

✔   Is the works cited information correct?

✔   Does your summary begin with an introduction clearly stating the author's primary focus?

✔   Does your summary's discussion section explain the author's *primary* contentions and omit secondary side issues?

✔   In the discussion section, do you explain the author's contentions through pertinent facts and figures while avoiding lengthy technicalities?

✔   Is your content accurate?  That is, are the facts that you've provided in the summary exactly the same as those the author provided to substantiate his or her point of view?

✔   Have you organized your discussion section according to the author's method of organization?

✔   Did you use transitional words and phrases?

✔   Have you omitted direct quotations in the summary, depending instead on paraphrases?

✔   Does your conclusion either reiterate the author's primary contentions, reveal the author's value judgment, or state the author's recommendations for future action?

✔   Is your summary completely objective, avoiding any of your own attitudes?

✔   Have you used an effective technical writing style, avoiding long sentences and long words?

✔   Are your grammar and mechanics correct?

✔   Have you avoided sexist language?

Source: **WRITTEN COMMUNICATIONS RESOURCE DIGEST**, Gurman, Page 258, 259

Insert Assignment in Part IV, Written Skills, S.K.I.P.

## Guideline 3-2
## Brainstorming Checklist

**PURPOSE:**

Brainstorming is a technique for generating as many ideas as possible in a short time period.

**GUIDELINES:**

- Establish understanding of the session's goal

- Promote relaxed environment

- Encourage all members of group to participate

- Encourage all ideas

    Be creative! Take a "try anything" attitude

- Write down all ideas

    If ideas are being given too fast for one person to write them down have two people writing or tape session.

- Do not criticize or evaluate any ideas

- Focus on quantity not quality

- Encourage people to build or "hitchhike" on others' ideas

- Encourage people to suggest similar ideas

- Encourage people to "piggyback" or put two ideas together to make a new idea

- Do not take time to discuss or clarify

- When ideas seem to stop be sure to wait before closing the brainstorming session

Insert Guideline in Part IV, Group Dynamics, S.K.I.P.

## Guideline 3-3
## Work Organization Considerations

**Highlight one phrase in each line that most closely correlates with your desired work environment.**

| 1 | 2 | 3 |
|---|---|---|
| **STRUCTURE** | | |
| Encourage to work independently | Provides limited supervision and guidance | Provides regular guidance and detailed instructions |
| Encourages and provides opportunity for creativity | Provides limited opportunity for creativity | Encouraged to follow company procedures |
| Encourages new systems for efficient operation | Has a procedure to recommend change | Stresses systematic and efficient operation |
| Individual expected to accomplish task but is allowed flexibility in work schedule | Individual has regular hours but is allowed some flexibility | All individuals work set hours with little or no lead way |
| Individual is given some choice as to projects he/she is assigned | Most work is assigned but individual may be allowed to give preference | All projects are assigned |
| **MANAGEMENT** | | |
| Little supervision. Individual meets overall performance standards or completes task | Supervisors make regular check of work completed. Focus on performance rather than method | Supervisor monitors work and methods on frequent bases |
| Positions are more functional than hierarchical | Levels of supervision based on reporting and organizational flow | Stresses positions, titles and status |
| Open communication at all levels | Chain of command recognized but all supervisors encourage open door policy | Communication strictly adheres to chain of command |
| Decisions made at the lowest possible level. Individuals empowered to make decision within their area of responsibilities | Individuals given limited areas of decision. Most decisions made by management team | Decisions made at the executive level and passed down |
| Quality teams and work teams have decision making powers. They are consulted on all related matters | Quality teams and work teams make and defend recommendations to supervisors. Final decision made by management team | Quality teams and work teams given guide procedures to follow. They make written reports to management. Management makes most decisions |
| Encourages risk taking | Sets parameters on risk | Discourages risk taking. Procedures must be followed |

Insert Guideline in Part VI, Employment Decision-Making, S.K.I.P.

## Guideline 3-3 (Continued)

| | | |
|---|---|---|
| Job descriptions are very general and focus on performance. Specific standards are agreed on by individual and their supervisor | Job descriptions focus on general methods and more detailed performance standards | Detailed job description and procedures provide individual with specifics of how to accomplish job |
| **CULTURE** | | |
| Easygoing harmonious work environment. Little stress | Some work related stress. Individuals help and support one another | Formal environment. High stress among workers |
| Individuals cooperative with little internal competition | Some friendly competition among workers and departments | Highly competitive between individuals and/or departments |
| High energy environment with fast pace | Varied environment with overall pace medium | Methodical environment. Pace deliberate |
| Individuals friendly and sociable | Individuals cordial, but little socialization during work time | Individuals discouraged from socializing during work hours |
| Socialize outside work hours. Company activities (company teams, picnics, parties, etc.) Planned and unplanned socialization crosses organizational levels | Little planned socializing outside work. Although peers may share lunch or some outside socializing, seldom crosses organizational levels | Any planned activities follow organizational levels with strong element of protocol |
| Provides positive rewards and compliments | Compliments superior accomplishments | Uses annual formal employee rating system |
| Focus on employees and develops abilities to match organizational needs | Focus on performance and provides limited help and retraining | Focuses on performance. Little or no training |
| Cares about welfare of employees. Have employee assistance, excellent benefit programs | Benefit programs goal is to keep and attract employees | Provide benefit programs as required by law |
| Measures employees according to their work relationships as well as performances | Focuses on employees as it relates to getting job done | Focuses on the performance, measures individuals in quantitative ways |

Insert Guideline in Part VI, Employment Decision-Making, S.K.I.P.

**Guideline 3-4**
**Reference Materials**

**"DICTIONARIES, ENCYCLOPEDIAS, AND OTHER REFERENCE MATERIALS"**
The following are sources for information concerning careers.

| DICTIONARIES, ENCYCLOPEDIAS AND OTHER REFERENCE MATERIALS | | |
|---|---|---|
| **SOURCE** | **PUBLISHER** | **TYPE OF INFORMATION** |
| Dictionary of Occupational Titles (DOT) | US Dept. Of Labor | Categorizes and briefly describes most known occupations in US economy |
| Occupation Outlook Handbook (OOH) | US Dept. Of Labor | Provides nature of work; working conditions; estimated number employed in job; training, other qualifications, and advancement; job outlook; earning; related jobs and sources of other information |
| Guide for Occupational Exploration (GOE) | US Dept. Of Labor | List occupations in 12 broad interest, 66 work groups and 348 subgroups giving abilities and adoptabilities for each |
| Encyclopedia of Careers and Vocational Guidance | J. G. Ferguson | Facts on 650 occupations with 115 technician careers |
| VGM's Careers Encyclopedia | National Textbook Company | List 180 descriptions with details on places of employment, advancement and other sources |
| Career Choices Encyclopedia: Guide to Entry Level Jobs | Walker and Company | List entry level jobs for college graduate and gives job outlooks, expansion, and technical advances. Also list employers by type and location, work experience and extracurricular activities that would benefit or would help get job |
| College Placement Annual | College Placement Council | List companies and type of college majors they most often recruit |
| Dunn and Bradstreet's Million Dollar Directory | Dunn and Bradstreet | List 100,000 companies with names, addresses, numbers of employees, and managers |

Insert Guideline in Part II, Systems That Work, S.K.I.P.

**Guideline 3-4 (Continued)**

| | | |
|---|---|---|
| Encyclopedia of Associations | Gale Research Company | 13,000+ associations for most every industry with names and addresses |
| Guide to American Directories | Klein Publication | List 5,200 directories |
| Moody's Complete Corporate Index | Moody | 20,000 corporations included in other Moody publications |
| Encyclopedia of Business Information Sources | Gale Research Company | Source book of other source books |
| National Directory of State Agencies | Cambridge Information Group | National Directory of State Agencies; list state agencies and their functions |
| National Trade and Professional Associations | Columbia Books | List of organizations |
| Standard and Poor's Register of Corporations, Directories and Executives | Standard and Poor | List over 40,000 corporations and the directories |
| Thomas Register of American Manufactures | Thomas Publishing | Listing of manufacture and products |
| US Industrial Outlook | US Dept. Of Commerce | Reviews and forecast for over 350 companies |

Insert Guideline in Part II, Systems That Work, S.K.I.P.

## Guideline 3-5
## Reference Materials

### PROFESSIONAL AND TRADE ASSOCIATIONS

| OCCUPATIONS | ORGANIZATION AND ADDRESS |
|---|---|
| Accountants | American Institute of Certified Public Accountants, 1211 Avenue of the Americas, New York, NY 10036 |
| Aircraft industries | Aerospace Industries Association of America, 1725 DeSales St., N.W., Washington, DC 20036 |
| Architects | American Institute of Architects, 1735 New York Ave., N.W., Washington, DC 20036 |
| Architects, landscape | American Society of Landscape Architects, 1750 Old Meadow Rd., McLean VA 22101 |
| Bankers | American Bankers Association, 90 Park Ave., New York, NY 10016 |
| Building trades | AFL and CIO Building and Construction Trades Dept., 815 16th St., N.W., Washington, DC 20006 |
| Chemists | American Chemical Society, 1155 16th St., N.W., Washington, DC 20036 |
| Data processors | Data Processing Management Association, 505 Busses Hwy., Park Ridge, IL 60068 |
| Electrical workers | International Brotherhood of Electrical Workers, 1200 15th St., N.W. , Washington, DC 20005 |
| Engineers, aeronautical | American Institute of Aeronautics and Astronautics, 1290 Avenue of the Americas, New York, NY 10019 |
| Engineers, agricultural | American Society of Agricultural Engineers, 2950 Niles Rd., St. Joseph, MI 49085 |
| Engineers, ceramic | American Ceramic Society, 4055 N. High St., Columbus, OH 43214 |
| Engineers, chemical | American Institute of Chemical Engineers, 345 E. 47th St., New York, NY 10017 |
| Engineers, civil | American Society of Civil Engineers, 345 E. 47th St., New York, NY 10017 |

Insert Guideline in Part II, Systems That Work, S.K.I.P.

**Guideline 3-5 (Continued)**

| | |
|---|---|
| Engineers, electrical | Institute of Electrical and Electronics Engineers, 345 E. 47th St., New York, NY 10017 |
| Engineers, industrial | American Institute of Industrial Engineers, 345 E. 47th St., New York, NY 10017 |
| Engineers, marine | American Society of Naval Engineers, Inc., 1012 14th St., N.W., Suite 807, Washington, DC 20005 |
| Engineers, mechanical | American Society of Mechanical Engineers, 345 E. 47th St., New York, NY 10017 |
| Engineers, radio | Institute of Electrical and Electronics Engineers, 345 E. 47th St., New York, NY 10017 |
| Hotel workers | American Hotel and Motel Association, 221 W. 57th St., New York, NY 10019 |
| Mechanics, refrigeration and air conditioning | United Association of Journeymen, Apprentices of Plumbing and Pipe Fitting Industries, 901 Massachusetts Ave., N.W., Washington, DC 20001 |
| Medical record librarians | American Medical Record Association, 875 N. Michigan Ave., Chicago, IL 60611 |
| Recreation workers | National Recreation and Park Association, 1700 Pennsylvania Ave., N.W., Washington, DC 20006 |
| Restaurant workers | National Restaurant Association, 1530 N. Lake Shore Dr., Chicago, IL 60610 |
| Secretaries | National Secretaries Association, 616 E. 63rd St., Kansas City, MO 64110 |

Insert Guideline in Part II, Systems That Work, S.K.I.P.

**Guideline 3-6**
**Reference Materials**

| NAME | ADDRESS |
|---|---|
| The Catapult on Jobweb | http://www.jobweb.org/catapult/catapult.htm |
| Career Mosaic | http://www.careermosaic.com/ |
| Career Web | http://www.cweb.com/ |
| Internet Online Career Center | http://www.occ.com |
| Occupational Outlook Handbook | http://stats.bls.gov/ocohome.htm |
| E-Span | http://.www.espan.com |
| America's Job Bank | http://.www.ajb.dni.us/index.html |
| About Work | http://.www.aboutwork.com |
| College Grad Job Hunter | http://.www.collegegrad.com |
| The Education and Career Center | http://.www.petersons.com |
| Internet Sites for Job Seekers, Employers | http://.www.ups.purdue.edu/student/jobsites.htm |
| Job Direct | http://.www.jobdirect.com |
| Job Web | http://.www.jobweb.org |
| Job Trak | http://.www.jobtrak.com |
| Student Center | http://.www.studentcenter.com/ |
| CareerNet | http://.www.careers.org/ |
| CareerPath | http://.www.careerpath.com |
| Career Site | http://.www.careersite.com/ |
| IntelliMatch | http://.www.intellimatch.com |
| JobCenter | http://.www.jobcenter.com |
| ProMatch | http://.www.promatch.org/ |
| Skills Search | http://.www.internet-is.com/skillsearch/ingnn.html |
| Career Magazine | http://.www.careermag.com/ |
| The Monster Board | http://.www.monster.com |
| The Riley Guide | http://.www.jobtrak.comm/jobguide/what-now.html |

Insert Guideline in Part II, Systems That Work, S.K.I.P.

**Guideline 3-6A**
**NEW REFERENCES**

Add additional references for future use.

| NAME | ADDRESS |
|------|---------|
|      |         |
|      |         |
|      |         |
|      |         |
|      |         |
|      |         |
|      |         |
|      |         |
|      |         |
|      |         |
|      |         |
|      |         |
|      |         |
|      |         |
|      |         |
|      |         |
|      |         |

Insert Guideline in Part II, Systems That Work, S.K.I.P.

## Guideline 3-7
## Visitation Reminders

### COMPANY VISITATION REMINDERS

✔   Make an appointment through Human Resource Department or Manager.

✔   Get clear directions as to the location of the company, where you should go, and with whom you are to meet.

✔   Write out a list of questions.

✔   Dress as you would for an interview.

✔   Be a few minutes early for the appointment.

✔   Speak clearly and listen carefully.

✔   If appropriate, take notes.

✔   Thank them in person.

✔   Prepare notes about your visit as soon as possible.

✔   Write a thank you note.

Insert Form in Part VII, Company Information, S.K.I.P.

**Form 3-1**
**Research Worksheet for Work Organizations**

Name:_____Date:_____

Choose a company or an organization in your local area where you could conceivably seek a job in an occupation ranked high among your prospects. Your research could focus on an entire company or institution, if it is small (approximately 50 to 100 employees). In the case of a large organization, you should concentrate on a division or department. In other words, limit the size of the unit you research. Otherwise, your investigation will be too general and the scope too broad.

1.　　　Name of organization_____

　　　　Address_____Telephone_____

　　　　Other locations_____

　　　　Approximate number of employees _____ Industrial category_____

　　　　Sources of information about the organization:

　　　　Titles of written sources:_____

| People Contacted (Names) | Address/Telephone | Dates Contacted | Interview |
|---|---|---|---|
|  |  |  |  |

　　　　Thank you letter sent:

　　　　Yes _____ When?_____

　　　　Name of person with hiring authority _____

　　　　Divisions/departments within organization_____

Insert Form in Part VII, Company Information, S.K.I.P.

**Form 3-1 (Continued)**

(Obtain or make an organizational chart. Indicate where you would fit in.)

In which department would I work?_____

What could I do for this organization?_____

2. Goods produced/services provided_____

Volume of business and share of market in area_____

3. Organizational culture or departmental subculture - type(s)_____

Values/beliefs_____

Customs/rituals/ceremonies_____

Clothing worn on the job_____

Physical setting_____

First impressions_____

Subjects highlighted in communications_____

General appearance of workplace_____

Are the values of the organization compatible with me?_____

Why?_____

4. Types of people in the organization_____

Are they compatible with me? Why?_____

5. Advancement opportunities_____

Next highest position on career ladder_____

**Form 3-1 (Continued)**

6. Wage/salary structure: Pay in my intended job (starting, average, top)_____

   Is this negotiable?_____ By what percent?_____

   Fringe benefits available_____


7. Educational/training opportunities_____


8. Special requirements to be hired_____


9. Impact of employment in organization on my family_____


10. Is location acceptable?_____


Compare to Form 1-13 in Part VI, Employment Decision Making.
Rate the organization from 1-5 (1 is low, 5 is high) based on your assessment of the above.

| ORGANIZATION NAME: | 1 | 2 | 3 | 4 | 5 |
|---|---|---|---|---|---|
| Match my values | | | | | |
| Match my income needs | | | | | |
| Match my skills | | | | | |
| Other factors important to me: | | | | | |
| * | | | | | |
| * | | | | | |
| * | | | | | |
| * | | | | | |
| TOTAL SCORE | | | | | |

Insert Form in Part VII, Company Information, S.K.I.P.

**Form 3-1**
**Research Worksheet for Work Organizations**

Name:_____ Date:_____

Choose a company or an organization in your local area where you could conceivably seek a job in an occupation ranked high among your prospects. Your research could focus on an entire company or institution, if it is small (approximately 50 to 100 employees). In the case of a large organization, you should concentrate on a division or department. In other words, limit the size of the unit you research. Otherwise, your investigation will be too general and the scope too broad.

1.  Name of organization_____

    Address_____Telephone_____

    Other locations_____

    Approximate number of employees _____ Industrial category_____

    Sources of information about the organization:

    Titles of written sources:_____

| People Contacted (Names) | Address/Telephone | Dates Contacted | Interview |
|---|---|---|---|
|  |  |  |  |

Thank you letter sent:

Yes _____ When?_____

Name of person with hiring authority _____

Divisions/departments within organization_____

**Form 3-1 (Continued)**

(Obtain or make an organizational chart. Indicate where you would fit in.)

In which department would I work?_____

What could I do for this organization?_____

2. Goods produced/services provided_____

Volume of business and share of market in area_____

3. Organizational culture or departmental subculture - type(s)_____

Values/beliefs_____

Customs/rituals/ceremonies_____

Clothing worn on the job_____

Physical setting_____

First impressions_____

Subjects highlighted in communications_____

General appearance of workplace_____

Are the values of the organization compatible with me?_____

Why?_____

4. Types of people in the organization_____

Are they compatible with me? Why?_____

5. Advancement opportunities_____

Next highest position on career ladder_____

Insert Form in Part VII, Company Information, S.K.I.P.

6.  Wage/salary structure: Pay in my intended job (starting, average, top)_____

    Is this negotiable?_____ By what percent?_____

    Fringe benefits available_____


7.  Educational/training opportunities_____


8.  Special requirements to be hired_____


9.  Impact of employment in organization on my family_____


10. Is location acceptable?_____


Compare to Form 1-13 in Part VI, Employment Decision Making.
Rate the organization from 1-5 (1 is low, 5 is high) based on your assessment of the above.

| ORGANIZATION NAME: | 1 | 2 | 3 | 4 | 5 |
|---|---|---|---|---|---|
| Match my values | | | | | |
| Match my income needs | | | | | |
| Match my skills | | | | | |
| Other factors important to me: | | | | | |
| * | | | | | |
| * | | | | | |
| * | | | | | |
| * | | | | | |
| TOTAL SCORE | | | | | |

Insert Form in Part VII, Company Information, S.K.I.P.

**Form 3-1**
**Research Worksheet for Work Organizations**

Name:_____ Date:_____

Choose a company or an organization in your local area where you could conceivably seek a job in an occupation ranked high among your prospects. Your research could focus on an entire company or institution, if it is small (approximately 50 to 100 employees). In the case of a large organization, you should concentrate on a division or department. In other words, limit the size of the unit you research. Otherwise, your investigation will be too general and the scope too broad.

1.     Name of organization_____

       Address_____Telephone_____

       Other locations_____

       Approximate number of employees _____ Industrial category_____

       Sources of information about the organization:

       Titles of written sources:_____

| People Contacted (Names) | Address/Telephone | Dates Contacted | Interview |
|---|---|---|---|
| | | | |
| | | | |
| | | | |

       Thank you letter sent:

       Yes _____ When?_____

       Name of person with hiring authority _____

       Divisions/departments within organization_____

**Form 3-1 (Continued)**

        (Obtain or make an organizational chart. Indicate where you would fit in.)

        In which department would I work?_____

        What could I do for this organization?_____

2.     Goods produced/services provided_____

        Volume of business and share of market in area_____

3.     Organizational culture or departmental subculture - type(s)_____

        Values/beliefs_____

        Customs/rituals/ceremonies_____

        Clothing worn on the job_____

        Physical setting_____

        First impressions_____

        Subjects highlighted in communications_____

        General appearance of workplace_____

        Are the values of the organization compatible with me?_____

        Why?_____

4.     Types of people in the organization_____

        Are they compatible with me? Why?_____

5.     Advancement opportunities_____

        Next highest position on career ladder_____

Insert Form in Part VII, Company Information, S.K.I.P.

172

**Form 3-1 (Continued)**

6.      Wage/salary structure: Pay in my intended job (starting, average, top)_____

       Is this negotiable?_____ By what percent?_____

       Fringe benefits available_____


7.      Educational/training opportunities_____


8.      Special requirements to be hired_____


9.      Impact of employment in organization on my family_____


10.    Is location acceptable?_____

Compare to Form 1-13 in Part VI, Employment Decision Making.
Rate the organization from 1-5 (1 is low, 5 is high) based on your assessment of the above.

| ORGANIZATION NAME: | 1 | 2 | 3 | 4 | 5 |
|---|---|---|---|---|---|
| Match my values | | | | | |
| Match my income needs | | | | | |
| Match my skills | | | | | |
| Other factors important to me: | | | | | |
|    * | | | | | |
|    * | | | | | |
|    * | | | | | |
|    * | | | | | |
| TOTAL SCORE | | | | | |

Insert Form in Part VII, Company Information, S.K.I.P.

**Form 3-1**
**Research Worksheet for Work Organizations**

Name:_____ Date:_____

Choose a company or an organization in your local area where you could conceivably seek a job in an occupation ranked high among your prospects. Your research could focus on an entire company or institution, if it is small (approximately 50 to 100 employees). In the case of a large organization, you should concentrate on a division or department. In other words, limit the size of the unit you research. Otherwise, your investigation will be too general and the scope too broad.

1.  Name of organization_____

     Address_____Telephone_____

     Other locations_____

     Approximate number of employees _____ Industrial category_____

     Sources of information about the organization:

     Titles of written sources:_____

| People Contacted (Names) | Address/Telephone | Dates Contacted | Interview |
|---|---|---|---|
|  |  |  |  |
|  |  |  |  |
|  |  |  |  |

Thank you letter sent:

Yes _____ When?_____

Name of person with hiring authority _____

Divisions/departments within organization_____

Insert Form in Part VII, Company Information, S.K.I.P.

**Form 3-1 (Continued)**

(Obtain or make an organizational chart. Indicate where you would fit in.)

In which department would I work?_____

What could I do for this organization?_____

2.      Goods produced/services provided_____

        Volume of business and share of market in area_____

3.      Organizational culture or departmental subculture - type(s)_____

        Values/beliefs_____

        Customs/rituals/ceremonies_____

        Clothing worn on the job_____

        Physical setting_____

        First impressions_____

        Subjects highlighted in communications_____

        General appearance of workplace_____

        Are the values of the organization compatible with me?_____

        Why?_____

4.      Types of people in the organization_____

        Are they compatible with me? Why?_____

5.      Advancement opportunities_____

        Next highest position on career ladder_____

---

Insert Form in Part VII, Company Information, S.K.I.P.

6. Wage/salary structure: Pay in my intended job (starting, average, top)_____

   Is this negotiable?_____ By what percent?_____

   Fringe benefits available_____

7. Educational/training opportunities_____

8. Special requirements to be hired_____

9. Impact of employment in organization on my family_____

10. Is location acceptable?_____

Compare to Form 1-13 in Part VI, Employment Decision Making.
Rate the organization from 1-5 (1 is low, 5 is high) based on your assessment of the above.

| ORGANIZATION NAME: | 1 | 2 | 3 | 4 | 5 |
|---|---|---|---|---|---|
| Match my values | | | | | |
| Match my income needs | | | | | |
| Match my skills | | | | | |
| Other factors important to me: | | | | | |
| * | | | | | |
| * | | | | | |
| * | | | | | |
| * | | | | | |
| **TOTAL SCORE** | | | | | |

Insert Form in Part VII, Company Information, S.K.I.P.

Insert Form in Part VII, Company Information, S.K.I.P.

178

**Form 3-2**
**Organizational Rating Chart -- Culture**

Name:_____Date:_____

### COMPANY RANKING, (1 is low, 5 is high)

| Organization: | 1 | 2 | 3 | 4 | 5 |
|---|---|---|---|---|---|
|  |  |  |  |  |  |
|  |  |  |  |  |  |
|  |  |  |  |  |  |
|  |  |  |  |  |  |
|  |  |  |  |  |  |
|  |  |  |  |  |  |
|  |  |  |  |  |  |
|  |  |  |  |  |  |
|  |  |  |  |  |  |
|  |  |  |  |  |  |
|  |  |  |  |  |  |

Insert Form in Part VII, Company Information, S.K.I.P.

**Form 3-3**
**Panel Discussion**

Name:_____ Date:_____

Course:_____

| PANEL MEMBER | COMPANY | POSITION |
|---|---|---|
|  |  |  |
|  |  |  |
|  |  |  |
|  |  |  |
|  |  |  |

List and briefly explain "revelations" or conclusions you had as a result of this panel,

Insert Form in Part VII, Company Information, S.K.I.P.

**Form 3-3 (Continued)**
**Panel Discussion**

## SUMMARY

| PANEL MEMBER | DETERMINING FACTORS OF SALARY | DETERMINING FACTORS OF PROMOTION | TYPES OF POSITION FOR MY BACKGROUND |
|---|---|---|---|
|  |  |  |  |
|  |  |  |  |
|  |  |  |  |
|  |  |  |  |
|  |  |  |  |

Insert Form in Part VII, Company Information, S.K.I.P.

**Form 3-4**
**Peer Evaluation Team Project**

Name:_____    Date:_____

Your major contribution:

| TEAM MEMBER | CONTRIBUTION |
|---|---|
|  |  |

Rank each team member according to their contribution: 1 - being given to the most valuable team member.

**Form 3-5**
**Group Process**

GROUP _____

EVALUATOR _____

## PROJECT EVALUATION FORM

Each student will evaluate the group process twice during the quarter. The first evaluation must be turned in anytime during weeks 2-6. The second must be turned in anytime during weeks 7-11.

Circle the number that best reflects your evaluation of your group. Include comments beneath each question.

1. There was regular and consistent participation by most members.
   Yes      1    2    3    4    5    6    7    No
   Comments:

2. Members showed signs of listening (paraphrasing, responding to points made, summarizing other's points, nodding).
   Always      1    2    3    4    5    6    7    Never
   Comments:

3. Members appeared to be prepared for the meeting.
   Prepared      1    2    3    4    5    6    7    Unprepared
   Comments:

4. Discussion was focused and stayed on the topic or task.
   Always      1    2    3    4    5    6    7    Never
   Comments:

## PROJECT EVALUATION FORM (Continued)

5.  Members' statements were clear, brief, and easy to follow.
    Always      1     2     3     4     5     6     7     Never
    Comments:

6.  Group appears able to use the best techniques or procedure for managing meeting focus.
    Always      1     2     3     4     5     6     7     Never
    Comments:

7.  Members' evaluations and criticism were phrased constructively.
    Always      1     2     3     4     5     6     7     Never
    Comments:

8.  Members appeared to work in a cooperative manner.
    Always      1     2     3     4     5     6     7     Never
    Comments:

9.  Members were willing to offer opinions, ask questions, and contribute to discussion.
    Always      1     2     3     4     5     6     7     Never
    Comments:

10. Evaluation of opinions, ideas, proposals, and information was thorough and carefully done.
    Always      1     2     3     4     5     6     7     Never
    Comments:

11. Relationships among members appeared to be friendly and respectful.
    Always      1     2     3     4     5     6     7     Never
    Comments:

---

Insert Form in Part IV, Group Dynamics, S.K.I.P.

## PROJECT EVALUATION FORM (Continued)

12. Members volunteered to perform group tasks.
    Always          1      2      3      4      5      6      7      Never
    Comments:

13. Members followed through with assignments.
    Yes             1      2      3      4      5      6      7      No
    Comments:

14. All members are contributing to the success of this group.
    Yes             1      2      3      4      5      6      7      No
    Comments:

15. The overall group process is working.
    Yes             1      2      3      4      5      6      7      No
    Comments:

---

Insert Form in Part IV, Group Dynamics, S.K.I.P.

Insert Form in Part IV, Group Dynamics, S.K.I.P.

# PART IV

# TECHNOLOGY

## Guideline 4-1

### APPROACHING THE TECHNICAL CURRICULUM

As you approach your technical courses, it will be helpful if you apply some of the following techniques:

✔      Analyze your syllabi to determine course expectations.

✔      Link technical know-how to day-to-day problems:
           Analyzing the situation
           Correcting the error

✔      Assess means of moving up in the technical world
           Investigating different opportunities in the technical world
           Determining factors of a higher salary
           Getting the promotion

✔      Demonstrating what you know

The following forms and guidelines are designed to help you apply these techniques.

## Form 4-1

### KEY QUESTIONS

| KEY QUESTION | YES/ NO | SYLLABUS OR INSTRUCTOR RESPONSE |
|---|---|---|
| How will the grade be determined? | | If due dates or test dates given, put in your planner. |
| Will the material in the class explain assigned reading? | | If yes, read text before you attend class. Write questions. Keep notes by chapter. |
| Will material in class only highlight assigned reading? | | If yes, read text before you attend class. Write questions. Keep notes by chapter. |
| Will the material in class give additional material from assigned reading? | | If yes, read text so you can use it as foundation for material. |
| Are test questions taken from:<br>a. readings;<br>b. material given in lecture;<br>c. class discussion;<br>d. class activities;<br>e. combination | | Outline chapters, write/answer questions.<br>Outline lecture, write/answer questions.<br>Write questions and answers from discussions.<br>Write questions and answers from activities.<br>Leave spaces in chapter outline for other material. |
| Are there tutorial or helpful materials in the LRC? | | If yes, arrange time to check it out. |
| Will there be tutoring or help sessions outside class time? | | If they are pre-scheduled make a note of time. |
| What are the instructor's office hours? | | Write in text or planner. |
| Can the instructor be called or contacted by electronic mail? | | Write numbers in text or planner. |
| Will study groups be established? | | If yes, write names and phone numbers in text or planner. |

Insert Form in Part II, Systems That Work, S.K.I.P.

**Form 4-2**
**Key Questions**

Name:_____    Date:_____

NOTE: For maximum performance, review Chapter 2 from **PATHWAY TO SUCCESS.**

| KEY QUESTION | YES/ NO | SYLLABUS OR INSTRUCTOR RESPONSE |
|---|---|---|
| How will the grade be determined? | | |
| Will the material in the class explain assigned reading? | | |
| Will material in class only highlight assigned reading? | | |
| Will the material in class give additional material from assigned reading? | | |
| Are test questions taken from: a. readings; b. material given in lecture; c. class discussion; d. class activities; e. combination | | |
| Are there tutorial or helpful materials in the LRC? | | |
| Will there be tutoring or help sessions outside class time? | | |
| What are the instructor's office hours? | | |
| Can the instructor be called or contacted by electronic mail? | | |
| Will study groups be established? | | |

Insert Form in Part II, Systems That Work, S.K.I.P.

**Form 4-3**
**Employer Technical Questions**

Name:_____ Date:_____

In the context of your program of studies, a potential employer will probably ask or test you on some of the following questions:

1.

2.

3.

4.

5.

6.

7.

8.

9.

10.

11.

12.

Should be prepared to demonstrate competency on all of these.

In addition, employers may ask other questions. Use your skills, knowledge and Investment Portfolio to collect information on the key concepts in each of your courses so that you can properly prepare for the interview/testing process.

Insert Form in Part V, Technical Skills, S.K.I.P.

**Form 4-3**
**Employer Technical Questions**

Name:_____ Date:_____

In the context of your program of studies, a potential employer will probably ask or test you on some of the following questions:

1.

2.

3.

4.

5.

6.

7.

8.

9.

10.

11.

12.

Should be prepared to demonstrate competency on all of these.

In addition, employers may ask other questions. Use your skills, knowledge and Investment Portfolio to collect information on the key concepts in each of your courses so that you can properly prepare for the interview/testing process.

Insert Form in Part V, Technical Skills, S.K.I.P.

**Form 4-3**
**Employer Technical Questions**

Name:_____  Date:_____

In the context of your program of studies, a potential employer will probably ask or test you on some of the following questions:

1.

2.

3.

4.

5.

6.

7.

8.

9.

10.

11.

12.

Should be prepared to demonstrate competency on all of these.

In addition, employers may ask other questions. Use your skills, knowledge and Investment Portfolio to collect information on the key concepts in each of your courses so that you can properly prepare for the interview/testing process.

Insert Form in Part V, Technical Skills, S.K.I.P.

**Form 4-3**
**Employer Technical Questions**

Name:_____ Date:_____

In the context of your program of studies, a potential employer will probably ask or test you on some of the following questions:

1.

2.

3.

4.

5.

6.

7.

8.

9.

10.

11.

12.

Should be prepared to demonstrate competency on all of these.

In addition, employers may ask other questions. Use your skills, knowledge and Investment Portfolio to collect information on the key concepts in each of your courses so that you can properly prepare for the interview/testing process.

Insert Form in Part V, Technical Skills, S.K.I.P.

## Guideline 4-2
## Key Concepts Review

Many employers give tests as part of their hiring process. Past graduates have told us that they felt like they forgot much of what they had learned. This activity will help you summarize important points as you complete each quarter. We cannot anticipate the questions you may be asked, but we can provide you with a tool that you can summarize key points, models, formulas and problems. Some instructors will give you these key points as they cover the material while others may wait until the final review. The instructor will simply state put this in your bank. The test bank ledger is a way of keeping this information together so that you can review it prior to taking an employment test.

This log may contain actual information you want to remember of you may wish to refer to a drawing or separate page. On the separate sheet write the date, quarter, course, reference title of drawing or concept, and page number. On the log sheet write date, quarter, course name, reference name for drawing or concept, and page number given to extra sheet.

### TEST BANK

Start Date __3/15/97__   End Date __6/6/97__          Page _1_ of ____

| DATE | QTR | COURSE | ENTRY AND KEY EQUATION/FORMULA | REFERENCE |
|------|-----|--------|-------------------------------|-----------|
| 3/15 | 1 | Electronics | Electronic schematic drawing of DC circuit | Notes, page 1 |
| 3/25 | 1 | Electronics | 1=V/R Ohm's Law | Grob pg. 70 Notes, bk 1 12 |
| 3/25 | 1 | | R=V/I is resistance | Grob pg. 73 Notes, bk 1 13 |
| 3/25 | 1 | | V=IR=Voltage | Grob pg. 73 Notes, bk 1 14 |

**Guideline 4-2 (Continued)**
**Key Concepts Review**

Name:_____  Date:_____

| DATE | QTR | COURSE | ENTRY AND KEY EQUATION/FORMULA | REFERENCE |
|---|---|---|---|---|
| | | | | |
| | | | | |
| | | | | |
| | | | | |
| | | | | |
| | | | | |
| | | | | |
| | | | | |
| | | | | |
| | | | | |

Insert Guideline in Part V, Technical Skills, S.K.I.P.

**Guideline 4-2**
**Key Concepts Review**

Name:_____    Date:_____

| DATE | QTR | COURSE | ENTRY AND KEY EQUATION/FORMULA | REFERENCE |
|------|-----|--------|-------------------------------|-----------|
|      |     |        |                               |           |
|      |     |        |                               |           |
|      |     |        |                               |           |
|      |     |        |                               |           |
|      |     |        |                               |           |
|      |     |        |                               |           |
|      |     |        |                               |           |
|      |     |        |                               |           |
|      |     |        |                               |           |
|      |     |        |                               |           |

Insert Guideline in Part V, Technical Skills, S.K.I.P.

**Guideline 4-2**
**Key Concepts Review**

Name:_____     Date:_____

| DATE | QTR | COURSE | ENTRY AND KEY EQUATION/FORMULA | REFERENCE |
|------|-----|--------|-------------------------------|-----------|
|      |     |        |                               |           |
|      |     |        |                               |           |
|      |     |        |                               |           |
|      |     |        |                               |           |
|      |     |        |                               |           |
|      |     |        |                               |           |
|      |     |        |                               |           |
|      |     |        |                               |           |
|      |     |        |                               |           |
|      |     |        |                               |           |

Insert Guideline in Part V, Technical Skills, S.K.I.P.

**Form 4-4**
**Trouble Shooting=Problem Solving**

Name:_____     Date:_____

| PROBLEM SOLVING EXERCISE | |
|---|---|
| STEP | YOUR RESPONSE |
| **1. State the problem clearly.**<br>(State a problem you haven't resolved.) | |
| **2. Analyze the problem.**<br>(How does this problem impact you?) | |
| **3. Brainstorm possible solutions.**<br>(Explore as many options as you can.) | |
| **4. Determine the criteria for your solution.**<br>(Name the measures you will use for determining the effectiveness of your solutions.) | |
| **5. Explore each solution.**<br>(Discuss the negative and positive effects of your ideas. Match them to the criteria.) | |
| **6. Choose and execute the solution you decide is best.**<br>(How will you apply the solution?) | |

Insert Form in Part V, Technical Skills, S.K.I.P.

**Form 4-4**
**Trouble Shooting=Problem Solving**

Name:_____     Date:_____

| PROBLEM SOLVING EXERCISE | |
|---|---|
| STEP | YOUR RESPONSE |
| **1. State the problem clearly.** (State a problem you haven't resolved.) | |
| **2. Analyze the problem.** (How does this problem impact you?) | |
| **3. Brainstorm possible solutions.** (Explore as many options as you can.) | |
| **4. Determine the criteria for your solution.** (Name the measures you will use for determining the effectiveness of your solutions.) | |
| **5. Explore each solution.** (Discuss the negative and positive effects of your ideas. Match them to the criteria.) | |
| **6. Choose and execute the solution you decide is best.** (How will you apply the solution?) | |

Insert Form in Part V, Technical Skills, S.K.I.P.

**Form 4-4**
**Trouble Shooting=Problem Solving**

Name:_____     Date:_____

| PROBLEM SOLVING EXERCISE | |
|---|---|
| STEP | YOUR RESPONSE |
| **1. State the problem clearly.** (State a problem you haven't resolved.) | |
| **2. Analyze the problem.** (How does this problem impact you?) | |
| **3. Brainstorm possible solutions.** (Explore as many options as you can.) | |
| **4. Determine the criteria for your solution.** (Name the measures you will use for determining the effectiveness of your solutions.) | |
| **5. Explore each solution.** (Discuss the negative and positive effects of your ideas. Match them to the criteria.) | |
| **6. Choose and execute the solution you decide is best.** (How will you apply the solution?) | |

Insert Form in Part V, Technical Skills, S.K.I.P.

**Form 4-4**
**Trouble Shooting=Problem Solving**

Name:_____ Date:_____

| PROBLEM SOLVING EXERCISE | |
|---|---|
| STEP | YOUR RESPONSE |
| **1. State the problem clearly.**<br>(State a problem you haven't resolved.) | |
| **2. Analyze the problem.**<br>(How does this problem impact you?) | |
| **3. Brainstorm possible solutions.**<br>(Explore as many options as you can.) | |
| **4. Determine the criteria for your solution.**<br>(Name the measures you will use for determining the effectiveness of your solutions.) | |
| **5. Explore each solution.**<br>(Discuss the negative and positive effects of your ideas. Match them to the criteria.) | |
| **6. Choose and execute the solution you decide is best.**<br>(How will you apply the solution?) | |

Insert Form in Part V, Technical Skills, S.K.I.P.

## Guideline 4-3
## Getting the Most From Speakers and Panels

Speakers, panels and field trips offer a great opportunity for insights into various industries, companies, and jobs. You will have opportunities to participate in these events during your ITT Tech Career. The following forms will help you better utilize information as a foundation for your job search.

---

Insert Guideline in Part V, Technical Skills, S.K.I.P.

**Form 4-5**
**Speaker Review**

Name:_____ Date:_____

SPEAKER REVIEW          ADDENDUM____          STUDENT HANDOUT

Reviewer's Name

SPEAKER IDENTIFICATION:

Name                                                Company

Position                                            Years with Company

Product/Service

Topic

THREE TO FIVE PRIMARY POINTS OF SPEAKER


WOULD I WANT TO WORK FOR THIS COMPANY? WHY OR WHY NOT?


DID THE SPEAKER DESCRIBE A POSITION THAT MATCHES MY
INTEREST/SKILLS? EXPLAIN.


LIST AND BRIEFLY EXPLAIN PRIMARY "REVELATIONS" OR
CONCLUSIONS YOU HAD AS A RESULT OF THIS SPEECH.

Insert Form in Part V, Technical Skills, S.K.I.P.

**Form 4-5**
**Speaker Review**

Name:_____ Date:_____

SPEAKER REVIEW      ADDENDUM_____      STUDENT HANDOUT

Reviewer's Name

SPEAKER IDENTIFICATION:

Name                                Company

Position                         Years with Company

Product/Service

Topic

THREE TO FIVE PRIMARY POINTS OF SPEAKER

WOULD I WANT TO WORK FOR THIS COMPANY? WHY OR WHY NOT?

DID THE SPEAKER DESCRIBE A POSITION THAT MATCHES MY
INTEREST/SKILLS? EXPLAIN.

LIST AND BRIEFLY EXPLAIN PRIMARY "REVELATIONS" OR
CONCLUSIONS YOU HAD AS A RESULT OF THIS SPEECH.

Insert Form in Part V, Technical Skills, S.K.I.P.

## Form 4-5
## Speaker Review

Name:_____ Date:_____

SPEAKER REVIEW       ADDENDUM____      STUDENT HANDOUT

Reviewer's Name

SPEAKER IDENTIFICATION:

Name                                 Company

Position                           Years with Company

Product/Service

Topic

THREE TO FIVE PRIMARY POINTS OF SPEAKER

WOULD I WANT TO WORK FOR THIS COMPANY? WHY OR WHY NOT?

DID THE SPEAKER DESCRIBE A POSITION THAT MATCHES MY
INTEREST/SKILLS? EXPLAIN.

LIST AND BRIEFLY EXPLAIN PRIMARY "REVELATIONS" OR
CONCLUSIONS YOU HAD AS A RESULT OF THIS SPEECH.

Insert Form in Part V, Technical Skills, S.K.I.P.

Insert Form in Part V, Technical Skills, S.K.I.P.

**Form 4-5**
**Speaker Review**

Name:_____ Date:_____

SPEAKER REVIEW            ADDENDUM____       STUDENT HANDOUT

Reviewer's Name

SPEAKER IDENTIFICATION:

Name                                      Company

Position                                  Years with Company

Product/Service

Topic

THREE TO FIVE PRIMARY POINTS OF SPEAKER

WOULD I WANT TO WORK FOR THIS COMPANY? WHY OR WHY NOT?

DID THE SPEAKER DESCRIBE A POSITION THAT MATCHES MY INTEREST/SKILLS? EXPLAIN.

LIST AND BRIEFLY EXPLAIN PRIMARY "REVELATIONS" OR CONCLUSIONS YOU HAD AS A RESULT OF THIS SPEECH.

Insert Form in Part V, Technical Skills, S.K.I.P.

**Form 4-6**
**Panel Discussion**

Name:_____ Date:_____

Course:_____

| PANEL MEMBER | COMPANY | POSITION |
|---|---|---|
|  |  |  |
|  |  |  |
|  |  |  |
|  |  |  |
|  |  |  |
|  |  |  |

✔ List and briefly explain primary "revelations" or conclusions you had as a result of this panel.

Insert Form in Part VII, Company Information, S.K.I.P.

**Form 4-6**
**Panel Discussion**

Name:_____ Date:_____

Course:_____

| PANEL MEMBER | COMPANY | POSITION |
|---|---|---|
|  |  |  |
|  |  |  |
|  |  |  |
|  |  |  |
|  |  |  |
|  |  |  |

✔ List and briefly explain primary "revelations" or conclusions you had as a result of this panel.

Insert Form in Part VII, Company Information, S.K.I.P.

**Form 4-6**
**Panel Discussion**

Name:_____  Date:_____

Course:_____

| PANEL MEMBER | COMPANY | POSITION |
|---|---|---|
|  |  |  |
|  |  |  |
|  |  |  |
|  |  |  |
|  |  |  |
|  |  |  |

✔ List and briefly explain primary "revelations" or conclusions you had as a result of this panel.

Insert Form in Part VII, Company Information, S.K.I.P.

## Form 4-6
## Panel Discussion

Name:_____  Date:_____

Course:_____

| PANEL MEMBER | COMPANY | POSITION |
|---|---|---|
| | | |
| | | |
| | | |
| | | |
| | | |
| | | |

✔ List and briefly explain primary "revelations" or conclusions you had as a result of this panel.

Insert Form in Part VII, Company Information, S.K.I.P.

**Form 4-7**
**Summary of Position Information**

Name:_____ Date:_____

| PANEL MEMBER | ADVANTAGES OF POSITION | HIRING FACTORS | SUCCESS FACTORS |
|---|---|---|---|
|  |  |  |  |
|  |  |  |  |
|  |  |  |  |
|  |  |  |  |
|  |  |  |  |

Insert Form in Part VII, Company Information, S.K.I.P.

## Form 4-7
## Summary of Position Information

Name:_____ Date:_____

| PANEL MEMBER | ADVANTAGES OF POSITION | HIRING FACTORS | SUCCESS FACTORS |
|---|---|---|---|
|  |  |  |  |
|  |  |  |  |
|  |  |  |  |
|  |  |  |  |
|  |  |  |  |

Insert Form in Part VII, Company Information, S.K.I.P.

**Form 4-7**
**Summary of Position Information**

Name:_____    Date:_____

| PANEL MEMBER | ADVANTAGES OF POSITION | HIRING FACTORS | SUCCESS FACTORS |
|---|---|---|---|
|  |  |  |  |
|  |  |  |  |
|  |  |  |  |
|  |  |  |  |
|  |  |  |  |

Insert Form in Part VII, Company Information, S.K.I.P.

## Form 4-7
## Summary of Position Information

Name:_____ Date:_____

| PANEL MEMBER | ADVANTAGES OF POSITION | HIRING FACTORS | SUCCESS FACTORS |
|---|---|---|---|
| | | | |
| | | | |
| | | | |
| | | | |
| | | | |

**FORM 4-8**
**Field Trip Report Form**

Name:_____     Date:_____

| EMPLOYER NAME, ADDRESS, PHONE | TYPES OF POSITIONS | NUMBER OF EMPLOYEES |
|---|---|---|
| | | |
| | | |
| | | |
| | | |
| SUMMARY | | |
| | | |
| | | |
| MY INTEREST IN COMPANY | | |
| | | |
| | | |

| EMPLOYER NAME, ADDRESS, PHONE | TYPES OF POSITIONS | NUMBER OF EMPLOYEES |
|---|---|---|
| | | |
| | | |
| | | |
| | | |
| SUMMARY | | |
| | | |
| | | |
| MY INTEREST IN COMPANY | | |
| | | |
| | | |

Insert Form in Part VII, Company Information, S.K.I.P.

**FORM 4-8**
## Field Trip Report Form

Name:_____     Date:_____

| EMPLOYER NAME, ADDRESS, PHONE | TYPES OF POSITIONS | NUMBER OF EMPLOYEES |
|---|---|---|
|  |  |  |
|  |  |  |
|  |  |  |
|  |  |  |
| SUMMARY |  |  |
|  |  |  |
|  |  |  |
| MY INTEREST IN COMPANY |  |  |
|  |  |  |
|  |  |  |

| EMPLOYER NAME, ADDRESS, PHONE | TYPES OF POSITIONS | NUMBER OF EMPLOYEES |
|---|---|---|
|  |  |  |
|  |  |  |
|  |  |  |
|  |  |  |
| SUMMARY |  |  |
|  |  |  |
|  |  |  |
| MY INTEREST IN COMPANY |  |  |
|  |  |  |
|  |  |  |

Insert Form in Part VII, Company Information, S.K.I.P.

## FORM 4-9
## Demonstrating Technical Knowledge

Name:_____ Date:_____

**NOTE: Employers will expect you to demonstrate what you can do. This form will help you prepare for the interviewing process and will serve as an ongoing list of the key skills you have learned.**

| SKILL | EXAMPLE |
|-------|---------|
|       |         |
|       |         |
|       |         |
|       |         |
|       |         |
|       |         |
|       |         |

**FORM 4-9**
**Demonstrating Technical Knowledge**

Name:_____  Date:_____

**NOTE: Employers will expect you to demonstrate what you can do. This form will help you prepare for the interviewing process and will serve as an ongoing list of the key skills you have learned.**

| SKILL | EXAMPLE |
|-------|---------|
|       |         |
|       |         |
|       |         |
|       |         |
|       |         |
|       |         |
|       |         |

Insert Form in Part V, Technical Skills, S.K.I.P.

## FORM 4-9
## Demonstrating Technical Knowledge

Name:_____ Date:_____

**NOTE:** Employers will expect you to demonstrate what you can do. This form will help you prepare for the interviewing process and will serve as an ongoing list of the key skills you have learned.

| SKILL | EXAMPLE |
|-------|---------|
|       |         |
|       |         |
|       |         |
|       |         |
|       |         |
|       |         |
|       |         |

Insert Form in Part V, Technical Skills, S.K.I.P.

227

## FORM 4-9
## Demonstrating Technical Knowledge

Name:_____  Date:_____

**NOTE: Employers will expect you to demonstrate what you can do. This form will help you prepare for the interviewing process and will serve as an ongoing list of the key skills you have learned.**

| SKILL | EXAMPLE |
|---|---|
|  |  |
|  |  |
|  |  |
|  |  |
|  |  |
|  |  |
|  |  |

## FORM 4-9
## Demonstrating Technical Knowledge

Name:_____ Date:_____

**NOTE: Employers will expect you to demonstrate what you can do. This form will help you prepare for the interviewing process and will serve as an ongoing list of the key skills you have learned.**

| SKILL | EXAMPLE |
|---|---|
|  |  |
|  |  |
|  |  |
|  |  |
|  |  |
|  |  |
|  |  |

Insert Form in Part V, Technical Skills, S.K.I.P.

## FORM 4-9
## Demonstrating Technical Knowledge

Name:_____     Date:_____

**NOTE: Employers will expect you to demonstrate what you can do. This form will help you prepare for the interviewing process and will serve as an ongoing list of the key skills you have learned.**

| SKILL | EXAMPLE |
|-------|---------|
|       |         |
|       |         |
|       |         |
|       |         |
|       |         |
|       |         |
|       |         |

Insert Form in Part V, Technical Skills, S.K.I.P.

## FORM 4-9
## Demonstrating Technical Knowledge

Name:_____  Date:_____

**NOTE: Employers will expect you to demonstrate what you can do. This form will help you prepare for the interviewing process and will serve as an ongoing list of the key skills you have learned.**

| SKILL | EXAMPLE |
|-------|---------|
|       |         |
|       |         |
|       |         |
|       |         |
|       |         |
|       |         |
|       |         |